B.A.D. Medicine:

Trade treaties, privatization and health care reform in Canada

Jim Grieshaber-Otto

and Scott Sinclair

2004

CCPA
CANADIAN CENTRE
for POLICY ALTERNATIVES
CENTRE CANADIEN
de POLITIQUES ALTERNATIVES

Library and Archives Canada Cataloguing in Publication

Grieshaber-Otto, Jim

Bad medicine : trade treaties, privatization and health care reform in Canada / Jim Grieshaber-Otto and Scott Sinclair.

Includes bibliographical references.

ISBN 0-88627-402-8

1. Health care reform—Canada. 2. Canada—Commercial treaties—Social aspects. 3. Medical policy—Canada. 4. Privatization—Canada. 5. Health planning—Canada. I. Sinclair, Scott II. Title.

RA412.5.C3G75 2004 362.1'0971 C2004-903350-6

cover design by Studio 2 (studio2@rogers.com)

text layout & design by Dirk Van Stralen

Printed and bound in Canada

Published by

Canadian Centre for Policy Alternatives
Suite 410, 75 Albert Street
Ottawa, ON K1P 5E7
Tel 613-563-1341 Fax 613-233-1458
http://www.policyalternatives.ca
ccpa@policyalternatives.ca

CCPA
CANADIAN CENTRE
for POLICY ALTERNATIVES
CENTRE CANADIEN
de POLITIQUES ALTERNATIVES

SCEP 145 IGOI

CAW 567 OTTAWA

Contents

Acknowledgements

THE AUTHORS THANK Bruce Campbell, Corina Crawley, Colleen Fuller, Pierre Laliberté, Stan Marshall, Blair Redlin and Matthew Sanger for their advice and valuable suggestions on the manuscript. Any errors or omissions remain the responsibility of the authors. We are also grateful to Bruce Campbell, Kerri-Anne Finn, Ed Finn and Dirk VanStralen for the assistance they provided in bringing the book to publication.

This study was done by the Canadian Centre for Policy Alternatives (CCPA). We are grateful to the members of the CCPA's Trade and Investment Research Project, including the Canadian Union of Public Employees and the Canadian Labour Congress, for their ongoing financial assistance and support.

Finally, we wish to express our appreciation to Diane Exley and Rosalind Waters who, in countless ways, make our work possible.

Summary

THE CANADIAN HEALTH CARE SYSTEM is at a crossroads. One of the central and recurring themes in the debate over its future is whether private financing and for-profit delivery of health care should play a greater role in Canada as it does in our giant neighbour to the south.

An examination of Canada's international trade treaty obligations, and the scope of the exemptions for health care under those treaties, adds a crucial dimension to this important debate. It reveals that Canada's trade treaty commitments threaten to make commercialising reforms much more difficult and costly to reverse: basically a one-way street.

Three key reports on health care reform

Three major government-sponsored commissions have recently proposed blueprints for future health care reform in Canada. These are:

- **The Mazankowski report** (the Report of the Alberta Premier's Advisory Council on Health, chaired by former Deputy Prime Minister Don Mazankowski, published in 2001);
- **The Kirby report** (the recommendations of the Standing Senate Committee on Social Affairs, Science and Technology, chaired by Senator Michael Kirby, published in 2002); and

- **The Romanow report** (the report of the Commission on the Future of Health Care in Canada, chaired by former Saskatchewan Premier Roy Romanow, published in 2002).

These reports contain frequently opposing recommendations about the Canadian health care systems' financial sustainability, the values upon which the system is and should be based, and how the health care system should be reformed.

This study examines how implementing the reports' recommendations could interact with Canada's trade and investment treaty obligations. In particular, this study investigates the risk that the North American Free Trade Agreement (NAFTA) and the General Agreement on Trade in Services (GATS) could 'lock-in' privatization and market-oriented health care reforms, and impede the expansion of Medicare. It also examines the health care implications of negotiations that are now underway to extend the reach of the GATS and to conclude a Free Trade Area of the Americas (FTAA) treaty.

All of the three major reports take strong positions on the appropriate role of private financing and for-profit delivery of health care services. Both Mazankowski and Kirby clearly regard Canadians' substantial investment in health care as a rich commercial opportunity for the private sector. Both assert that subjecting the health care sector to entrepreneurial values and market discipline is necessary to modernize it. Mazankowski envisages a significantly expanded role for both private financing and for-profit delivery, while Kirby generally adheres to the principle of public financing (even envisioning expanding the medicare monopoly to new services) while embracing market-based mechanisms and an expanded private sector role in delivery.

Romanow, by contrast, vigorously supports renewing Medicare around the key principles of public financing and not-for-profit delivery. The Romanow report advocates a significant expansion of the public insurance monopoly to cover new services, strongly rejects a for-profit role in the delivery of core health services, and suggests that the inroads already made by for-profit providers in key areas such as diagnostic services be rolled back. Yet even Romanow, in a concession to the forceful privatization lobby, leaves the door open to an expanded private sector role in the delivery of so-called ancillary health services, which could include food services, cleaning services, maintenance services, computer and data management services, administration, and many other services that are critical to the health care system.

Increased involvement by foreign corporations brings increased risk of trade treaty challenges

From a trade treaty perspective, implementing the Romanow approach of promoting public, non-profit delivery of core health care services would generally reduce the likelihood of successful trade treaty litigation against Canada. By contrast, if implemented, the Mazankowski and Kirby proposals encouraging greater reliance on private for-profit corporations—including foreign corporations—in the Canadian health care system would increase the risk of trade treaty challenges.

Key trade treaty risks

Canada's medicare system is at odds with the principles of so-called free trade treaties. By establishing a public sector health insurance monopoly, and by regulating who can provide health care services and on what terms, the *Canada Health Act* and the medicare system cut against the grain of trade and investment liberalization.

While Canadians have repeatedly been assured that the health care system is beyond the reach of free trade treaties, in fact, Canada's health care system is only partially shielded from their force. While the treaties provide some critical protection, the safeguards fall short of the full "ironclad" exemptions for health repeatedly promised to Canadians.

The most serious free-trade threat is that, once entrenched in Canada, foreign health-care insurers and companies can make use of the North American Free Trade Agreement's (NAFTA's) tough expropriation-compensation rules. These provisions, which are broader than related Canadian domestic law, apply fully to Canada's health-care sector and are backed up by NAFTA's notorious investor-to-state dispute settlement process. They risk making experiments with for-profit health care essentially irreversible.

Another threat stems from Canadian negotiators' decision in 1994 to cover private health insurance under the World Trade Organization's trade-in-services agreement (the GATS). This reckless decision means that U.S. or European governments could challenge the expansion of our public health insurance system into new areas, such as pharmacare or homecare, by complaining that their private insurers were being denied market access. A GATS dispute could result in trade sanctions against Canadian exports to Europe or the U.S. The mere prospect of litigation could dissuade Ottawa from implementing such reforms.

While real, these risks can still be navigated around and should not be used as a pretext to thwart health care reform and renewal in Canada.

Commercialization at the provincial level heightens trade treaty risks

These risks, however, could soon become unmanageable. Several provincial governments are heightening trade treaty risks by facilitating the increased involvement of foreign corporations in Canada's health care system. This development, if left unchecked, poses one of the greatest risks to Medicare and to the success of future health care reform in Canada.

A number of provincial governments have recently promoted health care privatization. Numerous specific examples, which are collated in this study, illustrate the range of health care privatization that is now underway. They includes the establishment and maintenance of for-profit:

- Hospitals and clinics,
- Surgery, diagnostic and other specialized services,
- Administration, food, cleaning and other health-related services,
- Home-care, retirement home and assisted living services.

These forms of privatization foster the encroachment of foreign, for-profit companies into the Canadian health care system and steadily increase the risk of expensive trade treaty litigation to reverse the trend in the future. Regrettably, most local health authorities and governments at all levels – and Canadian citizens generally – have little, if any, appreciation of the power of trade treaty rules to 'lock-in' health care commercialization.

Under international trade treaties, federal support for public-private partnerships (P3s) risks distorting Canadian health care policy

Since coming into office, the federal Liberal administration under Prime Minister Paul Martin has exhibited an unprecedented enthusiasm for public-private partnerships (P3s) by:

- Maintaining an active P3 office within Industry Canada;
- Appointing P3 proponents to key bureaucratic and political positions;
- Creating a new cabinet post with specific responsibility for P3s, and appointing to it a P3 enthusiast who claims that P3s are "the way government is going to be done."

A public-private partnership is an arrangement between the public and private sector for the purpose of delivering a project or a service that is traditionally provided by the public sector. In most P3 models, public services are turned over to private corporations to run as profit- seeking enterprises. The public then rents back the infrastructure or services through long-term leases.

Under trade treaties, P3s threaten to diminish governments' regulatory ability in vital areas of health care policy, to shift risk from the investor or service provider to the public, and to increase costs through trade fines or sanctions.

Looming challenges of even more expansive trade treaties

Despite the dangers that existing trade treaties already pose to health care reform, the federal government is promoting new and more expansive international trade treaties that would worsen this threat. Ongoing negotiations to expand the ***General Agreement on Trade in Services (GATS)*** entail constant pressure on governments for new, more extensive GATS negotiating commitments; pressure for new restrictions on domestic regulations; and for other GATS concessions. In negotiations for a ***Free Trade Area of the Americas*** agreement ***(FTAA)***, the Canadian government actively supports incorporating many of the most controversial features of the ***North American Free Trade Agreement (NAFTA)*** investment chapter, including: investor-state dispute settlement; broad expropriation-compensation provisions; minimum standard of treatment rules; and prohibitions against performance requirements.

Each successive set of multilateral, regional and bilateral trade and investment negotiations makes the task of protecting the existing Canada's health care system from erosion, and renewing it without fear of trade treaty litigation, more difficult. Each agreement sets precedents for more intrusive provisions in the next. These cascading negotiations subject Canada to continuous pressure to weaken or even remove vital exceptions and reservations for health care. If any future federal government gives in to this pressure, its decision would bind all future governments. Unless this harmful dynamic is changed, the further erosion of protection for health care becomes only a matter of time.

Towards *healthy* health care reform

Canadian governments retain the capacity to navigate the risks that international trade treaty provisions now pose to health care reform. But to do so successfully will require new initiatives on a range of policy fronts.

Avoiding commercialization of health service financing and delivery—and taking prompt action to contain or reverse existing commercialization— is not only good public policy; it has the benefit of reducing the risk of future trade treaty challenges.

As a crucial first step, *governments at all levels should not proceed with so-called public-private partnerships in health care and should avoid P3 arrangements in the future.* Instead, governments should take measures to strengthen the public, not-for-profit character of the Canadian health care system which, if taken promptly, would insulate Canadians from future trade treaty challenges.

Health reforms should be fashioned to make the most benefit of existing safeguards by:

- Extending universal access to services on the basis of need, rather than ability to pay or other criteria;
- Establishing clear public purpose objectives and regulations;
- Financing services out of public revenue;
- Favouring direct subsidies or grants over contracted services; and

- Where services are contracted, adopting standard government procurement procedures.

Furthermore, from a trade treaty perspective, the sooner the widely-supported reforms to expand public insurance to new services such as homecare or prescription drugs occur, the better.

While health care commercialization in Canada is clearly proliferating, its scale is still limited, and the level of foreign involvement is smaller still. As a result, Canada's exposure to foreign investors' and service providers' treaty claims is, in most instances, not yet that extreme. Canada has a window of opportunity to reverse commercialisation and to expand its public health insurance system, but unless action is taken soon that window could close.

Towards a more balanced approach to international trade treaties

It is generally acknowledged that the NAFTA expropriation and compensation provisions pose the most serious trade treaty threat to Canadian health reforms. Less widely understood is that Canada's GATS commitments covering heath insurance are also a serious obstacle to the future expansion of public health insurance coverage.

Both these problems need to be remedied:

- Canada should negotiate a binding interpretation of NAFTA's investment chapter to narrow the meaning of expropriation to be consistent with that under Canadian law.
- If Canada fails to get agreement to do so from other NAFTA parties, it should strongly assert its own view that expanding public health insurance is not a compensable expropriation under domestic or international law and that NAFTA's investment rules will not be permitted to interfere with Canadian health care reforms.

- Canada should abandon its support of the NAFTA investor-state dispute settlement mechanism and instead seek its elimination in NAFTA and in bilateral investment treaties.
- Canada should withdraw its existing GATS commitment covering health insurance. The GATS Article XXI provides a means for countries to withdraw commitments upon negotiating "compensatory adjustments" in its GATS coverage. The sooner Canada invokes this process, the less difficult and costly it will be.

The Canadian health care system is a mixed public-private system. An overarching goal in negotiating trade and investment treaties must be to preserve the ability of governments to closely regulate Canada's entire mixed health care system: including its public; private, not-for-profit; and private, for-profit components. Governments' ability to shift this mix – without fear of becoming entangled in trade disputes and threat of sanctions – should be fully protected.

Canada should begin to champion new international health protection treaties that supersede commercial trade agreements. In the short term, the federal government must change its current approach so that the trade treaties it negotiates do not perpetually increase commercializing pressure on Canada's health care system. It should begin by securing the strong, fully effective protection for Medicare that Canadians were promised, but not given.

CHAPTER 1

Introduction

CANADA'S HEALTH CARE SYSTEM is a defining feature of modern Canadian life and our most valued social program. But its condition could soon become unstable. The current system is eroding through chronic under-funding and its nature is being altered by steady, incremental commercialization.

Canada's trade treaty obligations risk making such incremental changes effectively permanent, foreclosing important options for future reform. These trade treaty risks are not the only challenge facing the Canadian health care system. But no serious proposal to reform Canadian Medicare can afford to ignore them. They are a potentially corrosive and destabilizing influence that must be confronted and contained in order to secure the future of Canada's Medicare system.

The goals of this book then are: to explain and analyse these trade treaty risks; to assess the major proposals for Canadian health care reform through a trade treaty lens; to suggest practical steps to strengthen medicare that minimize the risks of trade treaty litigation; and to propose new approaches to international treaties and negotiating strategies that would better safeguard health care systems and their reform.

The concern over the future of our health system has generated much debate in recent years. In particular, three major government-sponsored commissions have proposed blueprints for health care reform. These reports are:

- The Mazankowski report (the Report of the Alberta Premier's Advisory Council on Health, published in 2001);
- The Kirby report (the recommendations of the Standing Senate Committee on Social Affairs, Science and Technology, published in 2002); and
- The Romanow report (the report of the Commission on the Future of Health Care in Canada, published in 2002).

The reports, however, contain frequently opposing recommendations about the Canadian health care systems' financial sustainability, the values upon which the system is and should be based, and how the health care system should be reformed. Also, two of the reports fail to even consider the health care implications of Canada's trade treaty commitments.

In effect, the three reports prescribe conflicting courses of treatment for an under-funded system already stressed by increasing doses of commercialization. The destabilizing interaction of trade treaty obligations with the growing trend towards commercialization in the Canadian health care system is too often neglected. This study aims to remedy that potentially dangerous oversight.

This study examines the significance of international trade treaty rules to the Mazankowski, Kirby and Romanow reports' recommendations on health care reform in Canada. It examines how the various proposals to increase competition and commercialization in the health sector would affect the risk of trade litigation. The study investigates the risk that the

North American Free Trade Agreement (NAFTA) and the General Agreement on Trade in Services (GATS) could 'lock-in' privatization and recommended market-oriented health care reforms. It also examines the health care implications of negotiations that are now underway to extend the reach of the GATS and to conclude a Free Trade Area of the Americas (FTAA) treaty.

The study is organized as follows:

The next chapter, Chapter 2, describes the trade treaty provisions that are most relevant to health care reform, focusing on the NAFTA and the GATS. It examines the broad scope and coverage of these treaties, and explains that the health safeguards they contain only partially shield the Canadian health care system from their binding rules. The chapter describes several important provisions both treaties contain, and examines other rules that are unique to each.

Chapter 3 considers each of the three health care reports in turn. Drawing on key quotations from each report, it describes the general features of each report and examines specific recommendations that are most relevant to NAFTA and GATS rules. This chapter also highlights aspects of a recent paper on the Kirby and Romanow reports written by Queens University Professor Thomas Courchene and published by the Institute for Research on Public Policy.

Chapter 4 examines the health reports' reform proposals from the perspective of trade treaty rules. It draws attention to the underlying conflict between trade treaty principles and the principles of Medicare. The chapter considers the significance, under trade treaties, of reducing the scope of public insurance coverage, expanding private delivery of publicly-insured services; expanding private delivery of services that are not publicly-insured; and other initiatives—including market-based devolution, a health care timeliness guarantee, and care groups—that would expand private, for-profit health care delivery in Canada. In addition, the chapter appraises the significance of public-private partnerships (P3s) and telehealth in the context of trade treaties.

The chapter also surveys developments in the health care field that are currently underway in various parts of Canada that increase the risk of future trade treaty litigation. These practices include the establishment or expansion of: for-profit hospitals and clinics; for-profit surgery, diagnostic and other specialized services; for-profit administration, food, cleaning and other health-related services; and for-profit home care, retirement home and assisted living services.

Chapter 4 closes with a discussion of new challenges that could arise as trade treaties become even more expansive in the future as, for example, envisaged in ongoing negotiations to create a Free Trade Area of the Americas (FTAA) or to expand the coverage of the GATS.

Chapter 5, which concludes the book, recommends ways in which citizens and governments can reform and strengthen the Canadian health care system while minimizing risks of trade treaty challenges. The chapter focuses on enlarging Medicare coverage and expanding public, not-for-profit health care delivery. Finally, the chapter offers specific recommendations for changing governments' approach to trade treaties in order to relieve pressure on health care. It recommends altering certain treaty commitments, changing Canada's trade negotiating strategies, and re-balancing the privileges of private, commercial interests with citizens' fundamental right to health.

CHAPTER 2

Key trade treaty rules and health safeguards

2.1 Introduction

FEW WOULD DISPUTE that there is a fundamental incompatibility between Canadian medicare and the full force of international free trade and investment treaties. By establishing a public sector health insurance monopoly, and by regulating who can provide health care services and on what terms, the *Canada Health Act* and the medicare system cut against the grain of trade and investment liberalization.[1]

To manage this underlying contradiction and to allay public concern about the potential threat that commercial treaties pose to public health care, successive Canadian federal governments have emphatically pledged to keep health care "off the table." In all recent trade negotiations, Canada's stated objectives include guaranteeing its ability to maintain existing health measures and to adopt new health measures.

It is the efficacy of these safeguards that is at issue. They consist of a patchwork of exclusions, exceptions and reservations to the application of NAFTA and WTO trade rules, some of which apply generally to all nations and others that are specific to Canada. While they provide some critical protection, the safeguards fall short of the full "ironclad" exemptions for health repeatedly promised to Canadians. By how far is a matter of debate that may only finally be resolved through trade disputes.

The overlay of trade treaties makes reforming the Canadian health care system a considerably riskier matter. It is an uncomfortable, but inescapable, reality that every important change to Canadian health care policy must now be vetted to ensure that it does not unnecessarily expose the health system to trade treaty litigation and potentially crippling sanctions. From a health policy perspective, vigilance and precaution are essential to ensure that commercial trade treaties neither erode Canada's existing health care system nor interfere with health care renewal and reform.

From a health care reform perspective, Canada's most significant trade and investment agreements are the NAFTA — particularly its investment, services, monopolies, and intellectual property chapters — and the WTO agreements, particularly the GATS and the TRIPS.[2]

The basic rules of the parallel NAFTA and WTO agreements are similar, but their precise scope and application can vary significantly. Interpretation is not always straightforward and applying the rules to a specific set of policy facts can be difficult. Domestic policy-makers must be aware of all the key obligations and how they interact. As a rule of thumb, where different provisions overlap it is the most restrictive that applies.

The following summary briefly reviews the key trade treaty provisions and safeguards affecting Canadian health care policy.[3] First, it examines the scope and coverage along with the health safeguards of each trade agreement. It then examines, in turn, the key provisions affecting health that are common to both agreements, the provisions that are unique to the GATS and, lastly, the provisions unique to the NAFTA.

2.2 Key provisions, scope and safeguards

The scope of the NAFTA is extraordinarily broad. Its services and investment chapters are "top-down," meaning that they cover all measures in all sectors except those for which governments negotiate explicit exclusions. The scope of the GATS is similarly broad, covering all types of measures taken by governments that "affect" trade in services, and all the ways in which these services are supplied, including electronically. Similarly, the GATS covers all services, except those provided "in the exercise of governmental authority (see discussion below)." Certain GATS provisions — the most important of which is the Most-Favoured Nation rule — are top-down and apply across-the-board to all sectors. But, in contrast to NAFTA, the most forceful provisions of the GATS are "bottom-up," applying only to those sectors that governments specifically agree to cover. Canada has not made specific commitments covering direct "health services" as classified by the GATS.

Both treaties contain features that partially shield health services, but in neither case can these be relied upon to fully protect the Canadian health care system from the treaties' force.

In NAFTA, Canada negotiated two important "reservations," or country-specific exceptions, that shield government measures in the health sector from certain, but not all, of NAFTA's investment and services obligations. The first of these, Annex I, is a general reservation against certain of NAFTA's provisions that permits each of the three NAFTA parties to maintain all non-conforming provincial and state government measures[4] that existed when NAFTA came into force on January 1, 1994.[5] The Annex I reservation applies against the NAFTA national treatment (1102, 1202), most-favoured nation treatment (1103, 1203), local presence (1205), performance requirements (1106) and senior management and board of directors (1107) articles. The Annex I reservation is bound.[6] This means that the "existing, non-conforming measures" are subject to a legal ratchet; they can only be amended to make them more NAFTA-consistent. If a measure is eliminated or amended it cannot later be restored. In other words, the protection afforded by the Annex I reservation is designed to disappear over time.

Canada negotiated a second reservation that excludes the Canadian health care sector from certain, but not all, provisions of NAFTA's investment and services chapters. This reservation, NAFTA Annex II-C-9, is commonly called "the NAFTA social services reservation." It applies against the national treatment (1102, 1202), the services chapter's most-favoured nation treatment (1203), local presence (1205) and senior management and board of directors (1107) articles. The Annex II reservation is unbound. This means that it protects not only existing non-conforming measures, but allows Canadian governments to take new measures that would otherwise be NAFTA-inconsistent. The reservation, however, stipulates that any such measures must be related to health to the extent that it is "a social service established or maintained for a public purpose."[7] These terms, which are undefined and have been subject to sharply differing interpretations by the U.S. and Canadian governments,[8] create uncertainty about the scope of the Annex II reservation.

The GATS excludes services provided in the "exercise of governmental authority." But these are defined as services provided neither on a commercial nor a competitive basis (GATS Article I:3.c). Because Canadian health care is a mixed system with significant private financing and delivery of services, the governmental authority exclusion cannot be relied upon to protect the Canadian health care system from GATS rules. Canada's decision not to list direct health services under the GATS provides more substantial protection. Canada has, however, covered certain health-related services; most notable is its troubling decision to list health insurance under the GATS.[9]

Upon scrutiny, the purported safeguards do not fully exclude the Canadian health care system. There are serious gaps in their protective mesh. For example, NAFTA's extremely broad provisions against "expropriation" without compensation apply with full force to all sectors, including health. Moreover, even where safeguards apply to a health service, increasing the commercial or competitive element in the financing or delivery of that service narrows the scope of those safeguards and, consequently, increases the exposure of the health service to trade law restrictions.[10]

2.2.1 Provisions common to both the NAFTA and the WTO

Most-favoured nation (MFN) and national treatment (NT) rules

Non-discrimination on the basis of nationality is a core principle of the international trading system. But it is only since the advent of NAFTA and the GATS that it has been extended beyond trade in goods to apply to investment and services matters.[11]

The most-favoured-nation (MFN) treatment rule requires that governments extend the best treatment given to any foreign goods, investments, or services to all like foreign goods, investments, or services: or "favour one, favour all."[12] The national treatment rule requires that governments give foreigners the best treatment given to like Canadian goods, investments, or services. Even measures that are formally (de jure) non-discriminatory can violate these non-discrimination rules if they, in fact (de facto), adversely affect the "equality of competitive opportunities" of foreign investors or service providers.

The GATS MFN obligation (GATS Article II) applies fully to all sectors, including health care. The NAFTA Investment chapter's MFN obligation (Article 1103) also applies fully to health-related investment measures, except for those sub-national measures in effect as of January 1, 1994, which are shielded by the Annex I reservation.[13] The combined effect of these rules means that the best treatment that a government gives to any single foreign investor or service provider in the health care sector must be extended "immediately and unconditionally" to all like foreign investors and service providers in the health care sector.

Canada shielded those health policy measures existing on January 1, 1994 from the national treatment rules in both NAFTA's investment and services chapter (NAFTA Articles 1102 and 1202). Through Annex II-C-9, Canada also reserved the right to adopt or maintain health care measures that would otherwise violate national treatment, but only to the extent that they apply to health services that are "social services established or maintained for a public purpose."

The GATS national treatment rule (Article XVII) only applies to services that governments expressly agree to list. Canada has not listed most direct health services under the GATS, although it has covered health insurance. For scheduled services, the GATS national treatment obligation is more stringent because, unlike NAFTA's national treatment rules, it applies to subsidies.[14]

The extension of MFN and national treatment beyond trade in goods to matters once considered exclusive domestic policy prerogatives, raises new concerns for regulating the Canadian health care system. Because MFN already applies to the health care sector, the best treatment given to any single foreign investor or service provider in the health care sector must be given to all. Fortunately, the health care sector is still largely shielded from the national treatment rule. The Canadian health care system includes many policies that favour, directly or indirectly, locally based service providers. Such policies frequently exclude or disadvantage foreign service providers or investors.[15] Even non-discriminatory policies that favour not-for-profit providers, could be construed as de facto national treatment violations where not-for-profit providers are predominantly Canadian and commercial providers are predominantly foreign.

Rules on public monopolies and state enterprises

The GATS (Article VIII) and NAFTA (Chapter 15) restrictions on monopolies and exclusive service suppliers are broadly similar. Both agreements prohibit monopolies from "abusing their monopoly position" when competing in sectors outside their monopoly. Under the GATS, monopolies must be listed as country-specific exceptions in committed sectors or be eliminated. Under both agreements, a government wishing to designate a new monopoly in a covered sector may be required to provide compensation. In the case of NAFTA, monetary compensation is due where the creation of a monopoly is found to have expropriated a foreign investment. Under the GATS, a government must negotiate trade concessions to compensate foreign service providers for their lost market access, or face retaliation from the provider's home governments. [16]

These monopoly provisions raise concerns that expanding public health insurance might attract claims for compensation from foreign insurers under either or both of these agreements.[17] Furthermore, where public, non-profit providers such as hospitals "compete" with commercial entities, such as is now increasingly occurring with diagnostic radiology services, there is growing potential for a trade treaty claim that public providers are abusing their monopoly position by competing unfairly in sectors outside their monopoly.

Rules on government procurement

The NAFTA and the WTO Agreement on Government Procurement (AGP) are broadly similar. Both agreements set out detailed tendering procedures that must be followed in all government procurements over specified monetary thresholds. Both also prohibit local preferences, local sourcing and offsets (e.g. local content, technology transfer or local economic development requirements) for covered public purchases.

Neither the NAFTA procurement chapter nor AGP currently apply to procurement of health and social services. Moreover, neither NAFTA nor the AGP apply to local or provincial purchasing. Because of these exclusions, the current impact of these procurement rules on the Canadian health care system is minimal.

However, as noted in Chapter 4, some governments and local health authorities are employing new models of contracting such as public-private-partnerships (or P3s). These blur the line between government procurements, which are excluded from certain trade treaty provisions, and investments, which are not. If some of these new P3 contracting arrangements are deemed investments by trade dispute panels, then governments could lose the legal protection afforded by the procurement exceptions.

Rules on intellectual property rights

Both NAFTA chapter 17 and the WTO agreement on Trade-Related Intellectual Property (TRIPS) provide extensive protection for intellectual property, including patents on pharmaceutical products and processes. Both agreements require a minimum term of 20 years of monopoly patent protection from the date of filing a patent application (TRIPS Article 33 and NAFTA Article 1709(12)). Both agreements also provide exceptions for compulsory licensing regimes, although with certain conditions.[18]

The reduced availability of cheaper, generic drugs in the free trade era has had a dramatic effect on spending on drugs and overall Canadian health care costs. Between 1980 and 2001, spending on prescription drugs more than doubled from 5.8 to 12 per cent of total health spending in Canada.[19] Two WTO cases have further eroded Canadians' access to lower-cost generic drugs. In a WTO ruling in 2000, brand-name manufacturers won an extra three years of patent protection for drugs patented between 1987 and 1989. And in the same year, the WTO sided with the European Union in stripping Canadian generic drug manufacturers of the right to manufacture and stockpile generic drugs prior to the expiry of the patent (although Canada was able to defend its practice of "early working" where manufacturers test generic versions prior to the expiry of patents). These adverse rulings have been estimated to cost Canadian tens of millions of dollars in extra drug costs.[20]

2.2.2 Provisions unique to the GATS

Quantitative restrictions

GATS Article XVI , Market Access, prohibits governments from limiting the number of service suppliers or operations; the value of service transactions; or the number of persons that may be employed in a sector. Such limits are prohibited, whether expressed "in the form of numerical quotas, or the requirements of an economic needs test." Monopolies and exclusive service suppliers are among the GATS-inconsistent restrictions on "the number of services suppliers." Article XVI also prevents governments from restricting the types of legal entities through which suppliers may supply a service or putting limits on foreign capital participation. Governments "shall not maintain or adopt" any of these quantitative restrictions "either on the basis of a regional subdivision or on the basis of its entire territory."[21] Article XVI applies to all scheduled sectors.

This article is particularly troubling because it explicitly prohibits non-discriminatory government measures. In principle, national treatment is a relative restriction that allows each member government to adopt the policy it chooses (even if those differ from other members) so long as the measure is not discriminatory in law or in effect. By contrast, the GATS market access provision is framed in absolute terms. It precludes certain types of policies, whether they are discriminatory or not.

There is nothing quite like GATS Article XVI in other international trade treaties. The NAFTA services chapter, for example, simply requires federal governments to list non-discriminatory quantitative restrictions on the number of service providers or the operations of service providers in an annex. But the annex has no binding legal effect; the list is merely for transparency purposes.[22]

Canada has not committed most health services under the GATS. If it ever did so, a large number of common health care polices would be at odds with GATS Article XVI. Regional quotas on, for example, the number of health professionals, services per professional, on certain types of expensive diagnostic equipment, or on the total value of services that will be reimbursed under public plans are commonly used, or considered, as measures to control health care costs.[23] Furthermore, in the health and social services sectors, provincial and local governments frequently restrict subsidies or contracts for the private delivery of certain services to legally constituted non-profit providers. Applying Article XVI to the Canadian health sector would drive up health care costs and create policy chaos.

Restrictions on domestic regulation

Negotiations are now underway on the GATS Domestic Regulation provisions. Under GATS Article VI.4, members are negotiating the development of "any necessary disciplines" to ensure that licensing and certification, technical standards and certain other domestic regulation of services and service providers are, among other things, "not more burdensome than necessary to ensure the quality of the service." Pending the outcome of the negotiations under Article VI.4, GATS article VI.5 provisionally applies certain restrictions to measures in scheduled sectors. GATS Article VI is explicitly intended to restrict non-discriminatory regulation.

This article raises concerns that, in the event of a challenge, WTO panels will be positioned to second-guess domestic regulators regarding the optimal or most efficient way to regulate services. David Luff provides several examples of the types of health care measures that could be considered "more burdensome than necessary." These include: obliging health care providers to accept all patients rather than providing them with incentives to do so; restricting fees for service to ensure health care services are affordable rather than increasing social security payments to enable patients to afford the fee that is charged; cancelling licenses of doctors or health facilities for non-compliance with licensing conditions rather than using fines or publicizing lists of wrong-doers; or requiring hospitals or physicians to operate on a non-profit basis rather than controlling how they operate on a for-profit basis.[24]

The GATS domestic regulation negotiations underline again just how far trade negotiations have strayed from conventional trade issues. Health care systems, in Canada and around the world, are complex and highly regulated. Given the non-commercial values that underlie regulation in this sector, oversight by an international trade body committed to expanding commercial opportunities for foreign providers would be both highly problematic and fundamentally undemocratic.

2.2.3 Provisions unique to the NAFTA

Restrictions on performance requirements

Performance requirements are government measures that oblige investors to meet certain conditions, for example: to purchase locally; transfer technology; or to achieve other local economic development, environmental or social policy benefits. The NAFTA investment chapter prohibits governments from imposing or enforcing certain types of performance requirements "in connection with the establishment, acquisition, expansion, management, conduct or operation of an investment" (NAFTA Article 1106). Remarkably, Article 1106 bans not only those performance requirements placed on U.S. and Mexican investments, but also those on foreign investments of any nationality and even on Canadian investors.[25]

The NAFTA Annex II-C-9 reservation does not exempt performance requirements in the health care sector from Article 1106, the performance requirements' rules of NAFTA's investment chapter.[26] Also, while provincial and local government performance requirements that existed on January 1, 1994 are exempted under the Annex I general reservation, this protection does not apply to measures adopted after January 1, 1994. Consequently, all new performance requirements in the health care sector are exposed to challenge as potential violations of NAFTA Article 1106.

From a health policy standpoint, probably the most significant performance requirement prohibition is against requirements "to purchase, use or accord a preference to goods produced or services provided from persons in its territory." New measures requiring investors in the health care sector, whether domestic or foreign, to purchase, use or prefer goods or services within Canada could breach NAFTA Article 1106.[27] It is hard to reconcile this blanket prohibition (recalling that it applies to all investors and investments, including Canadians) with many commonplace health-care policies, such as provincial health plans not paying for health services provided outside their jurisdiction if the required services are available locally. Such policies are protected only to the extent that they existed when NAFTA came into force on January 1, 1994.

Minimum standard of treatment

The NAFTA investment chapter (Article 1105) requires host governments to treat foreign investors "in accordance with international law, including fair and equitable treatment and full protection and security." This seemingly innocuous obligation has been interpreted in rather unexpected ways by NAFTA investor-state tribunals. Tribunals have examined the administrative behaviour of governments towards investors and, in several instances, ruled that government officials have acted arbitrarily, in an untimely manner, or without sufficient transparency.[28] In some instances, damages have already been awarded for the breach of Article 1105.[29]

The NAFTA minimum standards of treatment rule has, in effect, created an exclusive right of administrative review for foreign investors that is directly enforceable through an international commercial arbitration process. This rule is not subject to any reservations. All administrative measures, including health-related measures, are therefore exposed to potential challenge.

Rules on expropriation and compensation

NAFTA rules on expropriation and compensation are particularly significant. Article 1110 provides that governments can expropriate foreign-owned investments only for a public purpose and only if they provide compensation according to NAFTA prescriptions.[30] The NAFTA's investment protection provisions can be invoked directly by investors through investor-state dispute settlement. Neither of Canada's NAFTA reservations for health care protects against expropriation claims under Article 1110.

Whether a particular measure is an expropriation, and the amount of compensation due to investors, are matters of interpretation to be determined by a NAFTA arbitral panel. Investors have successfully argued that non-discriminatory regulations that significantly diminish the value of their investments amount to expropriation under the treaty.[31] This is in sharp contrast to Canadian law, which generally does not regard non-discriminatory regulatory measures, for example legitimate land rezoning, to be expropriation.[32]

Of all the international trade treaty rules, this provision unquestionably poses the most serious threat to efforts to reform or renew the Canadian health care system. The "extremely broad definition of expropriation"[33] opens the door to NAFTA claims that measures to expand Medicare coverage or to restrict private for-profit provision of health care services amount to expropriation and that compensation must be paid to U.S. or Mexican investors that are adversely affected. Significantly expanding the public health care system into areas where substantial U.S. investment interests are already established will almost certainly trigger trade treaty litigation.

CHAPTER 3

Examining recent reports on health care reform

3.1 The Mazankowski Report

3.1.1 Introduction: Proposing radical change

In December 2001, the Alberta Premier's Advisory Council on Health issued its first report. Chaired by former Deputy Prime Minister Don Mazankowski, the Advisory Council recommended changes to Alberta's health system that it explicitly termed "fundamental". According to the Council, its report "sets out fundamental changes in how we should organize and deliver health services" (p. 5) and recommends "fundamental changes in how we pay for health services" (p. 4). The report's recommendations in each of three areas of health care—funding, organization and delivery—are indeed far-reaching and, as considered below, could have important trade-treaty-related ramifications.

3.1.2 The Mazankowski Report on funding: 'public funding is not enough'

A key premise of the Mazankowski report is that without fundamental changes, the current health system is financially unsustainable. The report reiterates this assertion vigorously:

> "Without changes, spending on health care is not sustainable." (p. 27)
>
> "Is Alberta's health system sustainable the way it is financed today? [T]he answer is almost certainly no." (p. 27)
>
> "[T]ax-financed health care in its current form is not sustainable." (p. 31).
>
> "Council members have come to the conclusion that the current health care system is not sustainable if it is solely funded from provincial and federal government budgets." (p. 53)

The report draws attention to the tension between the need for government to curb what it characterizes as "the trend for annual increases beyond what is affordable" and the need for adequate funding to meet increasing costs and demands. In doing so, the Council argues that new, private sources funding are required.

> "We know what we want from the health system. [W]e need to explore new ways of paying for it." (p. 5)
>
> "If we depend only on provincial and federal general revenues to support health care, we have few options other than rationing services." (p. 7)
>
> "We need to look at … diversifying the revenue stream so we're not solely dependent on the tax base or government budgets to support health care." (p. 40)
>
> "[W]e need to diversify the revenue stream…" (p. 31)

Such "diversification" means that the health care system would be funded proportionately less through general taxation and proportionately more from various forms of direct payments by citizens. According to the report, these options would include the following:

- introducing user fees (which the report notes would contravene the *Canada Health Act*)
- introducing variable premiums, deductibles or other forms of co-payments (which would also contravene the *Canada Health Act*)
- using the income tax system to 'tax' people for the health care services they use
- establishing a special health care tax
- implementing a form of medical savings accounts (p. 54).

Significantly from a trade standpoint, these options would also involve:

- "allowing privately funded and privately delivered health services" and
- "expanding supplementary or private insurance" (p. 54).

After examining each of the above options "on an initial basis", the report recommends the following health financing reforms:

- to increase health care premiums so that they make up 20% of the overall costs of insured services.[34] Furthermore, premiums should be tied to future increases in the costs of the health system and the scope of insured services. In other words, health premiums would increase correspondingly with the costs of insured services and "as new treatments, tests and services are added" (p. 61).
- that Medical Savings Accounts and variable premiums "have the most positive features and warrant further study." (p. 61)
- that Alberta continue to work with other provinces to develop joint purchasing schemes or a national formulary to control drug costs, and

- that Regional Health Authorities be allowed to raise revenues on their own. These revenues could come from charging fees for long-term care, implementing co-payments for home care, and charging fees for restaurant inspections, environmental assessments and public health education programs.[35]

3.1.3 The Mazankowski Report on organization and delivery: 'fundamentally change to expand the role of the private sector'

The report emphatically denounces the organization of the existing health care system, condemning it as an "unregulated monopoly"—a purported attribute it characterizes as a "serious flaw" (p. 4). In its blunt critique, the Council states that "[t]he system is organized by government, paid for by government, insured by government, and evaluated by government.... In short, it's a command and control system."(p. 21) Following this theme, and raising the spectre of the Cold War, the Mazankowski report declares that "[t]he old 'command and control' central planning approach doesn't work." (p. 21)

According to the Council, a fundamentally different approach is needed: "[i]t's time to open up the system ... take off the shackles ... [and] encourage competition and choice." (pp. 5, 25). In the section of the report entitled "The private sector has a role to play," the Council concludes that "[w]e need to seriously look at expanding the role of the private sector in delivering insured health services." (p. 25)

The Council's recommendations would make an expansion of private, for-profit health care—at the expense of the existing publicly funded and administered system—inevitable. While rarely explicit, the report strongly suggests that Medicare coverage should be reduced and that few, if any, new services or treatments should be publicly funded. The Council "strongly recommend[s]" a process be put in place "without delay" to decide "about what should and should not be publicly funded". (p. 45).

"If some services or treatments are taken off the list [of publicly insured services] or decisions are made that new treatments will not be added, those services could still be available in the health system but would be paid for [privately] through supplementary insurance, individual payments, or other approaches such as medical savings accounts." (p. 45)

Ominously implying a general threat to continued coverage of many health services that are now publicly insured, the report recommends that an expert panel should determine "whether all existing services should be 'grandfathered' for continued public funding" under the new regimen (p. 45). Also, new diagnostic treatments, services or drugs should be covered by public insurance "only if there are sufficient revenues from the province to cover the costs or if other, less useful or less effective services are removed from the list to free up the necessary resources." (p. 46, italics added) Moreover, the report recommends that "[a]ny new revenue approaches should give individuals more choices" (p. 53). "New sources of revenue should be used to enhance flexibility, encourage more options and choices in the system" (p. 54) in recognition of the need, according to the committee, for individual Albertans to "take more responsibility for their own health and the decisions they make." (p. 53).

The Council sometimes plays down the significance of its recommendations by emphasizing the theme of experimentation. It seems to suggest that the report's proposals would serve merely as pilot projects which, if they did not work, could be readily abandoned and their underlying policies reversed.

> "It's time to open up the system .... Allow health authorities to try new ideas ... and see what works and what doesn't." (p. 5).

> Recommendations include "encouraging and empowering health providers to explore and implement a number of different approaches to organizing and delivering health care services." (p. 8)
>
> "The Council consistently heard that there is a need to open up the system and try different ways of delivering services." (p. 22)

In a similar vein, the report includes an extract from an Edmonton Journal editorial: "private innovators could do wonders for our health care system." (p. 25).

The Mazankowski report's theme of experimentation does not bear scrutiny. As noted below, modern trade treaties undermine the role of experimentation in policy-making by making certain policy choices—including some of those Mazankowski proposes—effectively irreversible.

In any event, elsewhere in the report this theme is abandoned. Instead, the Council acknowledges that many of the changes it recommends would be more than mere one-off experiments or "a 'safety valve' to take pressure off the public system." (p. 23) Indeed, the report explicitly criticizes past health care innovation efforts on the basis that they suffered from "uncertain funding, high administrative costs and a heavy emphasis on evaluation" (p. 22) and because, as the report notes significantly, these pilots haven't resulted "in any fundamental change across the system." (p. 22).

The Mazankowski report clearly advocates the existing system be fundamentally and permanently altered. It proposes a radical restructuring of the current system—potential violations of the *Canada Health Act* notwithstanding—that the Council hopes could instigate sweeping change throughout the country.

"[T]he Council believes that Albertans have an opportunity to lead the country in true health reform. We have a well-earned reputation for tackling tough challenges, trying new approaches, and leading the way. Health is no exception." (p. 4)

3.1.4 Promoting health care commercialization and privatization

The report's basic approach to health care funding, organization and delivery is reinforced with specific recommendations that, if implemented, would promote increased commercialization and privatization of the health care system. From the standpoint of trade treaty obligations, commercialization and privatization are critical because they would almost certainly lead to increased foreign involvement in Canada's health care system and increase Canadians' exposure to future trade treaty challenges. The report advocates greater health care commercialization or privatization in several areas, as follows:

Breaking up Canada's "public monopoly" in health care; facilitating greater private involvement

Although it avoids plainly-worded recommendations on the subject, the Council indisputably advocates breaking up the existing system in favour of one with greater private involvement. The Council raises the prospect of, and later obliquely recommends, what it calls "unbundling" – separating different functions within the system.[36] This development would "expand ... the number of suppliers delivering health care services." (p. 48). The Council recommends that the health system should be "re-configure[d] [to] encourage more choice [...and] more competition." (p. 48) In explaining the "unbundling" option, the Council envisions a decreased government role:

> "Rather than have government act as the insurer, provider and evaluator of health services, the various functions could be broken up. The role of government could focus more on setting overall direction and allocating funding to health authorities." (p. 24)

The Council subsequently recommends that the government responsibility would be limited primarily to:

> "setting overall vision, goals and objectives for the health system" and

> "allocating funding to health authorities and other core functions". (p. 48)

It is ironic that the council recommends "unbundling" at a time when jurisdictions having extensive experience of it identify unbundling as a fatal flaw of privatization. The U.K. House of Commons Transport Committee, in its March 2004 report entitled The Future of the Railway, highlights "extremely serious systemic flaws in the present organization of the [privatized] railway" (p. 3)[37]. The Committee subjects the governments unbundling strategy to withering criticism:

> "**The constant theme throughout our work was the complaint that the current structure of the industry is too fragmented to provide clear lines of responsibility and leadership and a satisfactory basis for improved rail performance**." (pp. 5-6, bolding in original)
>
> "Our predecessor Committee highlighted the dangers of fragmentation in 2002, when it warned starkly that:
>
> 'The fragmentation brought about by privatisation contributed to the chaos and delay that paralysed the industry. It is essential that fragmentation is significantly reduced.'" (p. 6)
>
> "**[A]s the railway system is currently governed, there is no one organization capable of properly addressing the four questions with which we started. In our view, until there is a single body with the authority to deal with these questions, Government and the rail industry are condemned to spending energy debating structural issues rather than getting on and running the railway for the benefit of the traveling public and the country**." (p. 7, bolding in original)

The Mazankowski report, in advocating that the health care system in Alberta be "unbundled," is thus recommending the very approach that a subsequent all-party U.K. House of Commons Committee identifies as one of the key causes of the chaos that resulted from the privatization of the British Rail system. It is difficult to imagine how the Canadian system, once unbundled, could avoid what the U.K. Committee describes as "the appalling extent of the present confusion of responsibilities ..." (p. 6)

Promoting a greater role for regional health authorities

Under the Council's approach, health authorities would gain new powers to provide services either directly or through service agreements with public or private sector providers. This augmented role for regional health authorities is key to the Council's approach. Critically, this role could open the door to increased private—including foreign,for-profit health care delivery. The Council recommends that:

- "Regional health authorities would be given responsibility and authority for ... delivering and/or contracting for the delivery of a full range of insured health care services, and
- establishing service agreements with physicians, labs, private surgical facilities, clinics, groups of health care providers, and private [for profit] and not-for-profit organizations and agencies to provide health services, including primary health care" (p. 49; see also p. 7).

Health authorities would be authorized to contract with other health regions for certain health services (p. 50), to provide "joint administration" (p. 50), direct contracts with hospitals and, in the longer term, "alternative ownership arrangements and payment mechanisms" (p. 50). The Council approvingly cites a case of a European local authority that sold a hospital to a private company that now both owns and operates the facility (p. 25).

Establishing "care groups"

The Mazankowski report recommends the establishment of "care groups" (p. 52) organized on a "business" (p. 52) or "corporate model" (p. 67) to "market their services both to individual Albertans and regional health authorities and provide insured as well as uninsured health services." (p. 52; see also pp. 24, 67) While arguing that "a privately funded and privately delivered health system" "provide[s] the most choice, the report asserts, for the record, that "it certainly is not our preference" (p. 56) It does, however, recommend fundamental changes that would shift the existing heath care system in that direction: "an innovative blend of public and privately delivered health services—delivered under contract with regional health authorities and publicly funded." Moreover, the report leaves open the possibility that through the mechanism of "care groups," for-profit companies—including foreign companies or those having foreign affiliates—could become directly involved in many, if not all, aspects of the health care delivery system.

Health Care Guarantee: another potential route for expanding private, for-profit health care

The Council recommends that individual Albertans be guaranteed access to selected health services within 90 days. Under this scheme,

> "[i]f regional health authorities are unable to provide service within 90 days, they would have to consider other options for getting the service from another region or within a reasonable distance. Services could be arranged from either a public or private sector provider. If [regional health authorities were] unable to arrange services within 90 days, government would arrange for the services in another jurisdiction and

> the costs would be charged to the region where the patient lives." (p. 44)

This recommendation is significant because it would almost certainly lead to greater health care commercialization and increase the involvement of foreign, for-profit companies in the Canadian health care system.

Other recommendations involving increased commercialization or privatization

The council makes other recommendations that suggest, could lead to, or entail increased privatization or commercialization. These include the following:

- Publicly-insured services in private health care facilities

The Council reinforces its vision of public insurance and public and private delivery, stating:

> "As long as insured health care services are publicly funded and standards are in place, it should make no difference if services are delivered in public, private [for-profit], or [private] not-for-profit facilities."(p.51)

- Private information technology and services

The Council places considerable stock in information technology. It advocates the development of electronic health care cards for individuals which, in future, could facilitate medical savings accounts or a system of variable health care premiums. It expressly recommends governments and health authorities consider "contracts, leases, and public/private partnerships" (p. 47) as alternatives to developing or purchasing such technology. Where purchases are contemplated, it recommends giving consideration to systems "that have already been developed by private sector companies." (p. 47). Curiously, in light of its rejection of what it calls a "public monopoly" in health care, the Council contemplates a rigorously centralized approach in direction and standards for information technology, arguing that "regional health authorities should not have the option of 'going their own way'" in this important areas. (p. 47)

The Council recommends a review of the fee-for-service system to allow for payments to physicians for telephone consultations and for "remote consultations using telecommunications". While these recommendations may not seem particularly noteworthy now, the potential for "telehealth" and other services to be provided outside Canada may raise novel and important funding, confidentiality, and trade policy issues in the future.

- Public-private partnerships and other commercialization in research, products and services

The Mazankowski report underlines the importance of promoting "public/private partnership opportunities" for research generally (p. 8) and for health care information technology in particular (p. 70). It also promotes "commercialization of new products and services developed through health and medical research initiatives." (p. 8).

Such commercialization would not to be limited to research. As noted above, the Council recommends that individual regional health authorities (rather than the provincial government) be granted the authority to raise additional revenues independently. This is to be achieved by charging: higher fees for long-term care; co-payments for home care; and fees for restaurant inspections, environmental assessments and public education programs. The Council also recommends that

> "[Regional authorities] should also be encouraged to … market their expertise to other regions, other provinces and perhaps even to people in neighbouring states."

In fact, the Calgary Health Region (CHR) has adopted just this approach and has pursued contracts overseas to export health services. In September 2003, a private company under contract to the CHR was chosen as the preferred bidder in a multi-million dollar contract to provide management and health services in three outpatient surgical centres in London, England.[38] The proposed arrangement was controversial in part because because the company would draw staff from the NHS but also because the firm was to be paid more than the U.K. National Health Service (NHS) providers for equivalent services.[39]

Critically, according to the Canadian Medical Association Journal, the Calgary consortium expected "to export an undisclosed number of [Canadian] physicians, nurses and other health care workers to the UK"[40]—a move that inevitably would increase pressure on the Canadian health care system.

This high-profile deal collapsed in April 2004, however, when the U.K. Department of Health "deselected" the company from its preferred bidder status because it "could not offer value for money."[41] John Reid, the British secretary for health, told reporters that "If we had gone ahead with the Anglo-Canadian deal it would have cost ridiculously more than the NHS tariff for these [orthopaedic and general surgical] operations."[42] The company is reportedly still being considered to build a treatment centre in Southend, Essex.[43]

The Mazankowski report urges the development of independent, entrepreneurial regional health authorities, and fostering close commercial ties in the U.S. which could, as the Council states, "add considerably to the province's economy" (p. 69). Such an approach to expand exports would inevitably divert health authorities' attention away from their primary purpose of providing health care services to local residents. It would also change the ethos of the current health care system and, as considered below, could raise serious new trade treaty concerns.

3.2 The Kirby Report

3.2.1 Introduction

The Kirby report, released in October 2002, is the culmination of a two-year study on the state of Canada's health care system conducted by eleven senators of the Standing Senate Committee on Social Affairs, Science and Technology. The report was designed to examine the fundamental principles on which the system is based; its historical development, and the pressures and constraints it faces; the role of the federal government; and how the Canadian system compares with health care systems in other jurisdictions. This analysis of the Kirby report is concerned with volume six of the final report, which contains the committee's recommendations for health care reform in Canada.

3.2.2 Service-based funding, hospitals and private, for-profit delivery

The Kirby report proposes dramatic changes to the financing of hospitals and the organization of the services they provide. In particular, it recommends that within five years (p. 45) the various methods of hospital funding now in use in Canada—including line-by-line budgeting, population-based funding, global budgeting, and ministerial discretion—be eliminated in favour of service-based funding. Basically, this "service-based" funding approach would mean that rather than receiving an annual budget, hospitals would be funded based on the type and volume of the services they provide.

The report identifies enhanced "efficiency and performance" as a "particularly attractive characteristic" of the approach (p. 32). Service-based funding is intended to encourage hospitals to specialize and to "drive volume into the most efficient institutions."[44] Kirby also asserts that in health care "quality goes up as volume goes up."[45] The report notes approvingly the potential for service-based funding to lead to "hospitals becoming more independent from government" and to reductions in the size of provincial health departments with "a corresponding reduction in the number of their employees." (p. 38). Surprisingly, the report fails to analyse the potential for hospitals and local health authorities to become less accountable to the public as they become more independent of democratically elected governments.

Critically, for the purposes of this book, the committee also draws attention to the potential for service-based funding to accommodate different ownership structures. It states:

> "The combination of a single funder / insurer, service-based funding and the separation of funder and provider means that the funder is neutral on the issue of who owns a hospital. The funder / insurer would purchase the service from that institution offering the best price, provided that it met the necessary quality standards. Such an institution could be either publicly owned or owned by a private not-for-profit or for-profit organization." (p. 39)

The committee emphasizes that it is "neutral to the ownership question" (p. 54) and, more defensively, that it is "not pushing for the creation of private, for-profit, facilities" (p. 39). It argues that provided all institutions in a province "are paid the same amount for performing any given medical procedure or service" and "are subjected to the same rigorous, independent quality control and evaluation system" (p. 39),

> "the patient and the funder / insurer will be served equally no matter what the corporate ownership of a health care institution may be...." (p. 39, 54)

This line of argument, however, obscures, behind a literalistic reading of the *Canada Health Act*, the committee's advocacy of what would be a radical shift in the leitmotif of the health care system. The report protests that:

> "We have stated on numerous occasions, and we repeat it here again, that we are in favour of a single public funder/insurer for hospital and doctor services covered under the *Canada Health Act.*"

But the new funding model would quite deliberately lead to a psychological and cultural shift in which all hospitals would be encouraged to view patients as sources of revenue.[46] The report notes approvingly that under service-based funding:

> "...hospitals will adjust their service mix in order to earn the highest possible returns consistent with meeting the needs of the population they serve. Hospitals will be encouraged to specialize in those services they can do best, and those for which the rates of remuneration are most attractive; they will reduce to the point of not providing those low-volume services that are not, for them, appropriately funded." (p.40)

Whether such a shift violates the letter of the *Canada Health Act* is not the most critical issue. The recommended reforms set out to deliberately inject competition and market disciplines into a health care system that has been built around the primacy of the non-market values articulated, among other places, in the *Canada Health Act.*

The committee also dismisses evidence presented to it that patients are at higher risk of dying in investor-owned private for-profit hospitals and outpatient facilities than in their not-for-profit counterparts.[47] The McMaster University study explained the higher mortality rates by pointing to the pressures faced by investor-owned, for-profit operations to achieve rates of return expected by shareholders (typically 10-15%), pay high compensation to managers, and the requirements that they pay taxes. In short, "They must achieve the same outcomes as private not-for-profit institutions while devoting fewer resources to patient care."[48] The authors further point out that in a context, as currently in Canada, where extra-billing is prohibited such facilities would face a "daunting task" in meeting shareholder expectations without reducing the quality of care.

The Kirby Committee notes a number of methodological objections to the McMaster study by a University of Guelph economist and refers to another 1999 study that found that the standard of treatment in licensed and non-licensed homes for the aged in the Eastern townships of Quebec were "comparable." On this basis, it asserts that "Given the evidence in the literature, the Committee believes that leaving the *Canada Health Act* as it currently is – which means permitting private for-profit hospitals or clinics to operate under Medicare (since such institutions are not currently prohibited under the Act) – will not, as some critics maintain, weaken or destroy the health care system as we know it now." (p. 57)

As the committee's own estimates reveal, private for-profit hospitals have, to date, played only a marginal role in the delivery of publicly funded health care in Canada.[49] By intentionally removing one of the biggest obstacles to private, for-profit ownership of hospitals (that, with few exceptions, they are ineligible for core public funding), service-based funding would certainly increase the role for private, for-profit hospitals and specialised clinics. Indeed, the funding model is designed to readily identify those services where for-profit providers can turn a profit, providing "market research" for commercial providers looking to "skim the cream," by taking over the most lucrative services currently provided by the public and not-for-profit sector. By increasing the stake of commercial providers, such reforms would inevitably lead to increased presence in Canada of foreign commercial providers. As will be considered in Chapter 4, this would increase the stake of potential trade treaty litigants in the Canadian health care system, weaken Canada's current protections for health care under trade treaties, and make failed market-oriented reforms more difficult to reverse.

3.2.3 Devolving responsibilities for health services to regional health authorities

The Kirby report recommends that regional health authorities should be given more responsibility and authority for the full range of health services. That is, in addition to their current responsibility for hospital services in their regions, they would gain authority for physician services and prescription drug spending and thus be responsible for "delivering and/or contracting for the full range of publicly insured health services." (p. 73, italics added)

The new, more powerful regional authorities would also be charged with introducing "internal markets"—market-like mechanisms—into the health care system. Regional authorities would "hold the purse strings" and act as "purchasing agents" (p. 70). According to the Kirby recommendations, they would "be able to choose between providers (individual and institutional) on the basis of quality and costs" (p. 75) rather than "simply funding the decisions of those using the resources" (p. 70).

The Kirby Committee envisions regional health authorities as a key means for generating competition among hospitals, other institutions and individual health care providers:

> "There is opportunity to apply the rationale behind internal market reforms … through competitive contracts among the RHAs and the various public (RHA owned) hospitals. Competition can be further enhanced when private providers are allowed to compete with public providers for some publicly insured health services (such as day surgery and long term care)." (p. 71)

The report notes the current mode for remunerating doctors would need to be revised to achieve "a fully integrated system" (p. 72) where "[p]hysicians or groups of physicians should be able to choose the option of entering into contracts with RHAs or working outside the system." (p. 72) Kirby cites the Mazankowski report in claiming that RHAs are ready to take up this and other challenges. (p. 73)

Paradoxically, rather than acknowledging any ideological basis for its recommendations or the risk that regionalization and a market-based approach could, among other things, fragment the existing system, the committee asserts that these initiatives would "depoliticize" health care decisions and provide Canadians with "a truly seamless health care system." (p. 69)

The committee acknowledges that its market-based approach to health care devolution would "have to be achieved through other means in Ontario, the Yukon and Nunavut, since there are no RHAs in these jurisdictions" (p. 63) and that "internal markets ... cannot work properly in regions with a low population density." (p. 73) It also admits that "there have been few, if any rigorous assessments of the internal market reforms undertaken in other countries." (p. 75)

Despite these reservations, the committee emphasizes the importance of its recommendations, correctly noting their implementation would greatly increase the ability of regional bodies to influence the current health care system. Perhaps most importantly, the proposal would "solve" what the Committee considers "the current problem" of provincial governments exercising "top-down management" of the health care system. It would, according to the Committee, "ensure that RHAs have the necessary flexibility to reconfigure services in a way that is more in line with population needs" within a given region.

These recommendations are strikingly similar to those contained in the Mazankowski report. Indeed, this section of the Kirby report specifically credits Mazankowski, reiterating recommendations contained in that report (pp. 63, 73). While more subtle, the Kirby report also shares the Mazankowski report's view that governments role in the health care system should be curtailed sharply to that of merely providing oversight and funding. Kirby states:

> "The role of government should be that of overall system governance, setting policies with respect to the health of the population, negotiating strategic plans and budgets and funding RHAs to achieve their objectives." (p. 69)

For its part, according to Kirby, the federal government should "encourage" health care devolution to regional health authorities, and undertake initiatives—including the development of information systems, the evaluation of internal market initiatives and system outcomes, and the supply of human resources—specifically to support such market-based devolution of authority.[50]

Market-based devolution is a fundamental aspect of the Kirby report. The committee itself notes that several of its other recommendations are specifically designed to support the primary initiative of market-based devolution. For example, the committee calls for continued federal funding of information systems primarily because these systems would "make it possible to move to service-based funding for hospitals." (p. 75) "[S]ervice-based funding" for hospitals, in turn, is recommended at least in part because it would be required for "market-like incentives … to work." (p. 72) Similarly, the committee points out that "in order to be successful, internal market reforms require detailed and reliable costing information" (p. 74)—a subsidiary issue on which the committee makes recommendations elsewhere in its report. In short, the essential core of the Kirby report's view of health care reform is that government's administrative role should decline in favour of market-based devolution.

3.2.4 Establishing a "Health Care Guarantee"

Like the Mazankowski report, the Kirby report recommends establishing what it also calls a Health Care Guarantee. Under this scheme, a maximum waiting time would be set and made public for each type of major procedure or treatment. "When this maximum time is reached, the insurer (government) [would] pay for the patient to seek the procedure or treatment immediately in another jurisdiction, including, if necessary, another country (e.g., the United States)." (p. 117)

The Kirby Committee acknowledges that there is a "lack of data" on the length of time patients have to wait for particular services. (p. 110) Instead, it cites evidence of a "strong public perception" of a waiting list problem. (p. 110, italics added). It also cites two examples where "the creation of disciplined waiting lists in which patients receive treatment according to their priority of need and within a timeframe set by clinical guidelines" has, by itself, "alleviated and in many cases resolved ... [both] the problem of waiting and the perception that ... [waiting] times are too long." (p. 110)

Despite this acknowledged lack of evidence, and despite presenting evidence that new waiting list management techniques could alleviate the purported problem easily and cheaply, the committee rejects the notion that recommending a health care guarantee is "premature" (p. 113). At very least, the committee argues, "such a guarantee would serve as a spur to the creation of the necessary standards, criteria and information systems." (p. 113) Presumably, the committee believes that these developments would document the problem at issue and justify policy changes the committee already maintains are required.

Pressing ahead to justify its waiting time proposal, the committee pugnaciously insists that "governments must be made to bear the responsibility of their decisions":

> "[T]he blame for the waiting list problem should be placed where it belongs—on the shoulders of governments for not funding the system adequately, and jointly on governments and providers of health services... [G]overnments must pay for the remedy, namely patient treatment in another jurisdiction, while waiting list management systems are being developed and put in place." (p. 117)

Under this scheme, provincial governments, already suffering reduced federal health care contributions, would face the additional expense of paying for outside services, potentially at a much higher cost, for patients whose treatment is delayed largely for lack of adequate funding in the first place. Such a "Catch-22" system would divert a greater proportion of public monies to service providers located in the United States and other jurisdictions, or to foreign service companies and other private, for-profit providers in Canada. Not only would this scheme fail to address the underlying cause of the problem, under-funding, it would eventually make it much worse by mandating additional spending outside the local system at private market rates.

Even Romanow critic Thomas Courchene acknowledges that the proposed health care guarantee could prove to be "very expensive indeed." (see Section 3.4.2) In the U.K., under a wait-list system similar to the proposed health care guarantee, private hospitals have recently been criticized for charging the National Health Service greatly inflated fees for services provided specifically to reduce waiting times.[51]

The committee goes further, however, proposing a strong enforcement mechanism for the health care guarantee. According to the committee, the guarantee is so important that it is an outcome that the committee "insists must happen." (p. 120) It suggests the federal government enforce the guarantee throughout Canada by penalizing provinces for non-compliance:

> "When a patient exceeded the maximum waiting time, the federal government could then pay the cost of treating the patient in another jurisdiction, including in the United States, and deduct the cost from the cash it transferred under the CHST to the province in which the patient resides." (p. 120)

The committee rightly acknowledges that this approach would be "highly contentious" (p. 120). What it fails to note, however, is that the recommendation would exacerbate waiting time problems wherever provincial governments were unwilling or, especially where foreign services were much more expensive, unable to implement the health care guarantee. In these jurisdictions, the resulting reductions in federal funding could also further encourage the expansion of private, for-profit delivery. The initiative would also increase pressure for the very "parallel system of private delivery, financed by private insurance", that the committee professes to "passionately hope" does not emerge. (p. 120) Finally, by increasing, the number of Canadians treated in the United States and other foreign countries, this federal enforcement of a health care guarantee would further entangle Canada's health policy with the country's trade treaty obligations.

In a statement that seems to be at odds with the Committee's Health Care Guarantee proposal,[52] the Committee appears guardedly to open the door to private insurance for publicly funded services—in other words, a two-tier system:

> "[P]rivate insurance for publicly insured health services should continue to be disallowed, provided that such publicly insured services are delivered in a timely fashion." (p. p. 296, italics in original, underlining added)

This disturbing statement points to the committee's preference for private insurance for publicly insured hospital and doctor services that are not delivered promptly, however that is defined.

Despite this remarkable suggestion, the committee plays down the potential for its recommendations to lead a "two-tier" health care system in Canada. It states:

> "there is no reason why the private for-profit provision of publicly funded health services would result in a so-called 'two-tier' health care structure, as long as the *funding* of services remains *publicly* based and referrals to institutions continue to be determined by clinical need." (p. 54, italics in original, underlining added)

It is more likely, Kirby argues, that

> "private clinics would remain small and specialized. Such clinics would emerge in niches where their founders expect to be able to make a profit by operating at lower cost than the public system does, either by taking advantage of economies of scale or, as seems more likely, by taking advantage of economics of specialization." (p. 58)

The Kirby report fails to consider the potential for one or both of the criteria it mentions to not be satisfied—a result that adoption of the committee's own recommendations would make more likely.

With respect to the public funding criterion, for example, governments would face increased funding pressure as a result of the recommended Health Care Guarantee. They can be expected to reduce the number of services covered under public health insurance, and yield to increased political pressure to permit the greater use of privately-funded insurance. In a manner that closely echoes the Mazankowski report, Kirby notes this potential in Chapter 15:

> "In the event that additional money is not invested into health care ... or that government fails to ensure timely access to needed care, it is likely that there would be great pressure and ... probably a legal obligation on government, to let those Canadians who

> can afford to do so purchase private health care insurance to obtain privately delivered health services." (p. 266)

The committee's second criterion—referrals to health care institutions being based solely on need—is also doubtful, even incredible. The potential for corporate ownership links and shared profit motives, between health care providers, facilities and institutions and the well-known inclination of for-profit providers to limit care and avoid the very sick make it highly unlikely that referrals to institutions would "continue to be determined by clinical need" of patients alone.[53]

In effect, the Kirby report claims not to favour an increase in for-profit health care at the same time that it prescribes actions that could lead to just that—the proliferation of for-profit health care clinics, hospitals and services, an opening for private insurance for listed services, and, eventually, the development of a "two-tier" health care system in Canada.

Significantly, the Kirby report considers at length the potential, in the absence of prompt delivery of health services, for Charter challenges to be brought against laws that prevent individuals from obtaining faster treatment by personally paying for publicly-insured health services. (cf. Chapter 5) The report quotes extensively from an article on the Charter and health care by Stanley Hartt and Partrick Monahan.[54] According to Kirby:

> "Hartt and Monahan believe governments can do one of two things—governments can either finance and structure the publicly funded health care system in such a way that it provides timely access to medically necessary care, or they can allow Canadians to buy that care if such access is not available in the publicly funded health care system in a timely manner." (p. 106)

As already noted, Kirby's Health Care Guarantee would increase the costs of treatment, thereby adding to the financial pressures facing governments. Placed between this proverbial 'rock and a hard place', governments under Kirby's Guarantee would likely find the choice of private payments for publicly insured services the less unpalatable choice.

The Kirby Committee takes pains to appear objective about the outcome, claiming that it:

> "passionately hopes that it will not be necessary for unilateral action to be taken by the federal government or for a parallel system of private delivery, financed by private insurance, to emerge as a result of judicial decisions." (p. 120)

However, Senator Kirby and the committee have become far more directly involved in seeking to determine the outcome than the report suggests. In a startling development, Senator Kirby and nine other senators have directly intervened in a high-profile case that is now before the Supreme Court.

The case involves a doctor, Jacques Chaoulli, and his patient, George Zeliotis. As plaintiffs, they claim that the lack of timely access to publicly-insured health services, together with restrictions on access to privately-insured care, are violations of Section 7 of the Charter. The Quebec Superior Court rejected the Chaoulli claim, ruling that prohibiting individuals from purchasing private insurance for publicly-insured services could violate Section 7 rights of liberty and security of the person, but was nonetheless consistent with the principles of fundamental justice. According to Kirby, in making this judgment,

> "the Court sought to balance the right to purchase private health care insurance against the collective goal of ensuring equal access to medically necessary health services for all Quebec residents. To allow private health care insurance, in the court's view, would compromise the integrity, proper functioning and viability of the publicly funded health care system."[55]

Senator Kirby has intervened in the case in support of the effort to overturn the Quebec Superior Court decision that prohibited one of the plaintiffs from paying privately for a hip replacement—a publicly-insured service. In essence, Senator Kirby's intervention is intended to persuade the Supreme Court that private health care insurance for publicly-insured services should be allowed.

Aside from the substance of the intervention, Senator Kirby's involvement has sparked controversy for other reasons. The Canadian Health Coalition has argued that since Kirby is "a director of Extendicare Inc. … a for-profit nursing home chain … [his] corporate duties and responsibilities" conflict with his ability to "represent the merits of the case against for-profit health care."[56] Moreover, it is not clear on whose behalf Senator Kirby is appearing:

> "Is Mr. Kirby intervening on behalf of the Government of Canada? The Prime Minister of Canada? The Liberal Party of Canada? The people of Canada? Or the shareholders of Extendicare Inc.?"[57]

Senator Kirby's intervention raise even more fundamental questions. Senator Kirby and other members of the Committee originally sought to intervene in the Supreme Court case in their official capacity as Senators and members of the Standing Senate Committee on Social Affairs, Science and Technology. The Attorney General of Canada, in opposing the Senators' leave to intervene, stated:

> "The Attorney General of Canada does not consider it appropriate that the Senate or one [of] its committees as an institution, being an element of the Parliament of Canada … and therefore of the legislative process should obtain intervener status [in their official capacity]."
>
> "Senators have unique privileges and roles to play in the legislative process."

> "In the same way that individual judges, when acting in their judicial capacity may only do so through established avenues such as rendering decisions[,] our legal system provides for specific avenues for parliamentary action that serve to distinguish the parliamentary process from the judicial process."

Granting the Senators intervenor status in their official capacity "would create a whole new forum for political discussion incongruent with the proper functioning and role of Parliament by allowing a particular group of parliamentarians holding a particular point of view a second forum to make their case, without the balance of divergent legislators' views..."[58]

The Supreme Court ultimately granted the senators leave to intervene in the case, but only in their individual capacity.

In sum, the active involvement of Senator Kirby and other members of the Committee in the Chaoulli case before the Supreme Court raises serious questions about the Committee's professed opposition to two-tier health care in Canada. It also raises concerns about the accountability of Senator Kirby as both a public and private representative. Finally, as highlighted by the Attorney General of Canada, the case raises questions about the Senators' view of their proper role as parliamentarians.

3.2.5 Expanding insurance to cover catastrophic prescription drug costs

The Kirby report identifies the growing problem that many Canadians have inadequate insurance coverage against catastrophic prescription drug costs. The committee notes that the prescription drug costs have "increased faster than all other elements in health care" (p. 125) and that spending on prescription drugs accounts for a growing share of public health care expenditures. The *Canada Health Act*, however, does not apply to drugs used outside the hospital setting, and both provincial publicly-funded drug coverage and private insurance coverage vary widely within different parts of the country. The committee notes that for those citizens who have either public or private coverage, "there is substantial variation in .., [the] nature and quality" of that coverage. And "many Canadians have no coverage at all for prescription drugs." As a result, "[f]inancial hardship due to high prescription drug expenses is increasingly a real risk—indeed, it is a reality—for many individual and families in Canada." (p. 125)

The committee cites several factors driving rising drug costs: increased development and marketing costs; the potential for "enormously costly ... genetically tailored drugs"; greater use of drugs outside hospitals to treat chronic conditions; and the greater use of home care as cost drivers in the health care system. (pp. 127-8) Inexplicably, the Kirby Committee neglects to discuss the impact that changes to federal drug patent legislation, which critics have linked to negotiations on the NAFTA and the WTO intellectual property treaty (TRIPs), has had on escalating drug costs. The committee correctly concludes that "many Canadians incur high levels of prescription drug costs that were inconceivable only a few years ago." (p. 128)

In response to this growing problem, the committee pays particular attention to the most severe cases of high prescription drug expenses. It recommends that the federal government fund 90% of prescription drug expenses that are above a limit deemed "catastrophic" for individuals and families. The committee describes it proposal as follows:

> "[N]o one would ever be obliged to pay more than 3% of their family income for prescription drugs.

> Those who are members of a private [prescription drug insurance] plan that participates in the federal program would never pay more than $1,500 or 3% of their family income for prescription drugs, whichever is lower. Depending on whether or not an individual is a member of a private plan, the first $5,000 in total prescription drug expenses would be paid by some combination of individual out-of-pocket spending, public and private insurance. The federal government would then pay 90% of the prescription drug costs over $5,000 incurred by any individual in the course of a single year, with the remaining 10% of the costs over $5,000 being paid either by a provincial or a private supplementary plan." (p. 139)

Under this scheme, existing private supplementary drug insurance plans would not be obliged to participate in this federal program. In order to be eligible, however, these sponsors "would have to guarantee that no individual plan member would be obliged to incur out-of-pocket expenses that exceed $1,500 per year." (p. 142)

The committee also recommends the establishment of a "single national drug formulary", which is "necessary" to implement its expanded drug insurance plan "in a uniform and equitable manner across the country." (p. 143) Such a national formulary "could lead the way to the creation of a single national buying agency—one that covers all provincial/territorial/federal jurisdictions." Pooling individual jurisdictions' buying power in this way "would strengthen the ability of public prescription drug insurance plans to negotiate the lowest possible purchase prices from drug companies" and would "enable the funder of the program [the federal government] to exercise control over which drugs were eligible for coverage." (p. 143) This sensible proposal, to aggregate national buying power for drugs, stands in sharp contrast to the Kirby report's overall thrust to increase regionalization through devolution of responsibility and authority.

3.2.6 Expanding public insurance to cover post-acute home care; allowing contracting out of service delivery and monitoring

In a significant proposed expansion of the health-care safety net, the Kirby committee recommends "a national program to provide publicly funded insurance coverage for post-acute home care, that is, care for people requiring treatment at home following an episode of hospitalization." (p. 151) The committee emphasizes the growing need for home care:

> "The need for home care will become a major challenge as the baby boomers age, average life expectancy rises, health care delivery becomes both more de-institutionalized and more technologically complex, and as work and social patterns decrease the availability of informal care-giving by family members." (p. 145)

This limited national home care program, would be treated "as an extension of medically necessary coverage already provided under the *Canada Health Act*." (p. 159). It would apply to individuals receiving their first home visit within 30 days of their discharge from hospital and would continue for up to three months. The committee recommends that the full cost of the program "should be borne by government (shared equally by the provincial / territorial and federal levels)". (p.159) The program would include "nursing and therapy services" (p. 154) as well as "prescription drugs" (p. 155); indeed, the committee recommends that the range of covered "services, products and technologies ... not be restricted" (p. 155)

Kirby explicitly contemplates the contracting out of covered services, including to for-profit service suppliers:

> "The Committee recognizes that the method by which [post-acute home care] is organized and delivered is

> a separate question from how these services are funded, and that many different forms of service delivery are feasible. In some circumstances, hospitals may provide the services themselves; in others, hospitals may contract with not-for-profit or for-profit home care service providers; in yet other circumstances, hospitals may contract with third-party agencies that sub-contract with home care service providers." (p. 155).

The Committee ... recommends that:

> Hospitals have the option to develop contractual relationships directly with home care service providers or with transfer agencies that may provide case management and service provision arrangements." (p. 155)

The Kirby report recommends that however services are delivered—whether by hospital-based in-home service teams, or through contracting or sub-contracting delivery to a private agency—reimbursement should be "service-based". That is, "service providers [should] receive a flat rate for their services to a specific patient" (p. 156).

According to Kirby, this scheme, with fixed, predetermined payments, offers a number of advantages. These include the fact that "providers may retain residual income and ... have the incentive to select the most efficient ways of delivering services." Also, "vertical and horizontal service integration may occur" and, where payment exceeds the costs of providing services, service suppliers have an incentive "to compete for additional care recipients." (p. 156).

Kirby also identifies disadvantages of the proposal, namely that "this reimbursement method ... tends to encourage the avoidance of care recipients with high service needs, i.e., 'cherry-picking.'" In addition, "organizations may be tempted to skimp on service provision, potentially leading to diminished quality of care." (p. 156) Despite the seriousness of these disadvantages, the committee does not examine them further. Instead, it merely recommends that home care contracts should include unspecified "mechanisms to monitor service quality, performance and outcome." (p. 156) The logic of the report suggests that like service delivery, the service of *monitoring* home care service delivery could itself be contracted out to private domestic and foreign companies.

The Kirby home care proposal is especially noteworthy because it would facilitate and promote, within an expanded Medicare system, publicly-funded insurance for private, for-profit delivery of essential health care services.

3.2.7 Expanding public insurance to cover palliative home care

The Kirby report recommends that the federal, provincial and territorial governments develop a jointly-funded national palliative home care program. Unable to obtain the data necessary to estimate the cost of such a program, the committee recommends simply that the federal government agree to contribute $250 million per year toward developing the program. The committee proposes that caregivers receive financial assistance, tax credits and job protection but makes no recommendations on how the program should be organized. (Chapter 9) One can only surmise that the committee would likely recommend that the program should share key features of its proposal for a national program for acute home care services—including the potential for contracting out palliative home care service delivery.

3.2.8 Conclusion

The Kirby report supports a significant expansion of public health insurance to cover several new areas where needs are greatest: catastrophic drug coverage, post-acute long-term care and palliative care. The report does not consider how to overcome potential trade treaty obstacles to extending public health insurance to these new areas.

To its credit, the Kirby report also confronts the funding issue head on. It correctly attributes many of the problems of the health care system to cuts in federal transfers. Moreover, it does not try to absolve the federal government from its responsibility for this predicament. In stark contrast to the Mazankowski report which (even in resource-revenue-rich Alberta) calls for various initiatives to cap public spending on health, the Kirby report urges that the federal government commit a fixed portion of the Goods and Services Tax to health care transfers, thus ensuring that in future federal government contributions would grow with federal revenues.[59] Moreover, it recommends an additional federal contribution of $5B annually to expand Medicare coverage and as a vital prerequisite to reform and renewal.

This new federal infusion of cash would not come without strings. But, in an odd reversal, Kirby casts the federal role not in its traditional guise of safeguarding the non-profit principles of medicare against erosion, but as pushing for uniform, cross-country reforms to increase competition and promote greater use of market mechanisms in the health care sector.[60]

Indeed, these "pro-competitive" reforms are indisputably the centrepiece of the final Kirby report. Service-based funding is explicitly designed to promote the market values of competition and efficiency within the health care delivery system. And the substantial devolution promoted by the report would ensure that market-based "innovation" could occur more easily, freed from centralized administrative control, whether provincial or federal.

From a public policy point of view, the basic problem with the Kirby reforms, as with other market-inspired reform schemes, is that the "the most efficient way to make money in the health care business is to avoid sick people or to limit care",[61] manoeuvres that are clearly at odds with the underlying social values of the Medicare system. The Kirby report acknowledges this anti-social tendency of health care markets and proposes that quality controls (and various exceptions, for example for funding teaching and rural hospitals) be built in to the system to redress it. It also cites testimony that recognises the proclivity of profit-oriented providers to "game" the system and the concomitant need for strict administrative oversight to counter this. But bulking up administrative controls to counter the natural tendency of markets undermines one of the key strengths of the Medicare system—its administrative simplicity and efficiency. Where all patients are treated on the basis of need, costly administrative controls to prevent providers from spurning patients or limiting care are not required.

The Kirby report pointedly—and rather disingenuously—purports to be agnostic about private, for-profit delivery of publicly funded health care services. But, as noted above, he is intervening directly in support of it in a Supreme Court case.[62] There can be little doubt that the Kirby Committee proposals are intended, and Kirby's interventions are designed, to foster a greatly increased role for private for-profit delivery in Canada. From a trade policy point of view, as will be discussed in chapter 4, such increased commercialisation and greatly enhanced role of for-profit health care services raises the most troubling issues.

3.3 The Romanow Report

3.3.1 Introduction

The Romanow Commission, established in mid-2001, was mandated to dialogue with Canadians and to make recommendations to ensure "the long term sustainability of a universally accessible, publicly funded health system" in Canada. (Romanow report, Mandate, p. 1) The commission conducted extensive consultations and research and in November 2002 issued a final report that has been widely hailed as the most important report on Canadian health care in many years.

3.3.2 The Romanow Report's vision for medicare

Commissioner Romanow deliberately sets out the vision for the changes he recommends. As he stated when the report was released, his recommendations are intended to be:

> "based on a vision of medicare as a national endeavour, where governments work together to ensure timely access to quality health care services as a right of citizenship, not a privilege. And they are designed to achieve a more effectively integrated and more accountable world-class system that helps to make Canadians the healthiest people in the world." (November 28, 2002 statement, p. 2).

His overall aim is "to strengthen and modernize medicare, and place it on a more sustainable footing for the future." (Ibid., p. 2)

3.3.3 Sustainability of Canada's health care system

Romanow dismisses the claims commonly repeated by certain governments and health policy analysts that Canada's system of health care is no longer sustainable. According to Romanow,

> "Our health care system is adequately meeting our needs. Canada's health outcomes compare favourably with other countries and evidence suggests that we are doing a good job in addressing the various factors that impact on overall health. But there is room for improvement ... particularly for Aboriginal peoples and in the north."

He adds:

> "Meeting the needs of an aging population will add costs to our system, but these can be managed if we begin to make the necessary adjustments now."

Also:

> "Canada's spending on health care is comparable with other OECD countries and we spend considerably less per capita than the United States." (Executive Summary, p. xxiii).

He asserts, in contrast to Mazankowski and Kirby, that overall "Canada's health care system has served Canadians well and is as sustainable as Canadians want it to be." (Executive Summary, p. xxiii):

> "Governance involves the political, social and economic choices that Canadians, their governments, and those in the health care system make concerning how the system continues to balance the health services, health needs, and resources that make up the system." (Ch. 1, p. 2)

> "There is no 'invisible hand' that silently and unobtrusively keeps these elements in balance.... Maintaining the balance is, in fact, a deliberate act of will on the part of society." (Ch. 1, p. 2)

> "Ultimately, the question of whether and how the system is sustained comes down to choices by those who govern the health care system—by providers, by governments, by administrators and by Canadians themselves.) (Ch. 1, p. 2)

Romanow recommends a Canadian Health Covenant to serve as "a tangible statement of Canadians' values and a guiding force" for Canada's publicly funded health care system. (Executive Summary, p. xxiv) He outlines the five principles that have come to define the current system: public administration, universality, accessibility, portability, and comprehensiveness. (Ch. 1, p. 4) He proposes that the principle of comprehensiveness be "updated" and the principle of portability limited to "guaranteeing portability of coverage within Canada" (Exec. Summary, p. xxiv). A new principle—accountability—should be added to the *Canada Health Act* principles, and the scope of publicly insured services should be expanded.

3.3.4 Expanding public health care insurance coverage to include home care services

Romanow states that "a strong case can be made for taking the first step in 35 years to expand coverage under the *Canada Health Act*" (Ch. 8, p. 172) by including home care services. He indicates that home care "is one of the fastest growing components of the health care system." (Ch. 8, p. 171) and that a growing body of evidence indicates that "investing in home care can save money while improving care and the quality of life for people who would otherwise be hospitalized or institutionalized in long-term care facilities." (Ch. 8, p. 171)

The report notes that, because of the significant costs involved in providing home care services, "priorities should be placed on the most pressing needs… mental health, post-acute, and palliative care." It recommends coverage for "[h]ome mental health case management and intervention services", "[h]ome care services for post-acute patients, including coverage for medication management and rehabilitation services", and "[p]alliative home care services to support people in their last six months of life" (Ch. 8, p. 176). It further recommends that support, in the form of time off work and special benefits under Employment Insurance, should be provided to "the thousands of parents, loved ones, family and friends that provide direct support in the home." (Exec. Summary, p. xxxi; Ch. 8, p. 183-4)

3.3.5 Improving timely access to services

Like the Mazankowski and Kirby reports, the Romanow report emphasizes the importance of improving Canadians' timely access to quality health care services. Echoing the other reports, Romanow notes that this is "a serious challenge in every province and territory. Consistently, the Commission heard concerns from Canadians about waiting for diagnostic tests, waiting for surgeries or waiting to see specialists." (Ch. 6, p. 137). "Time and again," the report notes, "the Commission heard that, when it comes to access to specific diagnostic procedures and some surgical procedures, wait lists ... and waiting times ... are too long." (Ch. 6, p. 138)

While noting the importance of timely care from the perspective of citizens' health and quality of life, Romanow also draws attention to the negative impact long waits have on people's confidence in the nation's health system. When expectations on timeliness go unmet, "Canadians' faith in the health care system is undermined." (Ch. 6, p. 137). Indeed, Romanow observes, "[l]ong waiting times are the main, and in many cases, the only reason some Canadians say they would be willing to pay for treatments outside of the public health care system." (Ch. 6, p. 137)

But Romanow differs sharply with Mazankowski and Kirby both on the nature of the problem and proposed solutions. While affirming that "the problem is not just one of perception", Romanow rejects the notion that "the public system is no longer able to manage the situation (Ch. 6, p. 139)." This view, which is reflected in the Mazankowski and Kirby reports, "fail[s] to take into account the progress that is being made in some jurisdictions." (Ch. 6, p. 139) Moreover, he asserts, diverting patients away from the public system to reduce waiting times can worsen the situation:

> "private facilities may improve waiting times for the select few who can afford to jump the queue, but may

> actually make the situation worse for other patients because much-needed resources are diverted form the public health care system to private facilities." (Ch. 6, p. 139)

Romanow: 'approach health care guarantee with caution'

Romanow considers the Mazankowski and Kirby recommendations for "care guarantees" and concludes that they "should be approached with some degree of caution" (Ch. 6, p. 144.)

Firstly, Romanow states:

> "reliable methods are not available to determine what the appropriate guarantee should be and what the likelihood is that the health care system would be able to meet the time limits set in a guarantee."

They should "rely on an objective assessment of both the capacity of the system … and the urgency of the condition being treated. They cannot simply be pulled out of thin air and trumpeted to Canadians as a magic bullet solution." (Ch. 6, p. 144)

Secondly, Romanow distinguishes between life-saving and elective procedures:

> "Long waiting times for diagnosis and treatment of life-threatening medical conditions such as cancer and cardiac care are unacceptable. But the issue is different for elective surgeries or services that are not life-saving." (Ch. 6, p. 144)

He suggests that care guarantees could have perverse effects by reducing the flexibility that provincial and territorial health systems now have in managing elective procedures:

> "That flexibility could be lost if care guarantees were rigidly applied. It also would be unfortunate to see the provincial and territorial health care systems handcuffed into care guarantees for elective or non-life-saving services that could, in practice, mean they would have to reallocate resources away from life-

> saving surgery or treatment in order to meet the care guarantees for other services." (Ch. 6, p. 144)

In contrast to Mazankowski and Kirby, Romanow proposes a straightforward, pragmatic approach for reducing waiting times that would not involve increasing the involvement of private, for-profit and foreign service providers in the Canadian health care system.

He recommends a new federal Diagnostic Services Fund to "provide direct support to provinces and territories" to shorten waiting times for diagnostic services. (Ch. 6, p. 140) These federal monies—part of "targeted funds to kick-start needed changes in five key areas" (Romanow statement, p. 4)—should be used "on a priority basis" (Ch. 6, p. 140) to purchase equipment and train the necessary staff and technicians to make up for years of what Romanow calls "under-investment" (Executive Summary, p. xxix). The Commission expresses confidence that this can result in "immediate and tangible improvements" (Ch. 6, p. 140) and could "free up resources to be used to address pressing access problems in other areas." (Ch. 6, p. 140)

Romanow also proposes that wait lists be managed more effectively. After citing examples of encouraging initiatives that are underway to achieve this (Ch. 6, pp. 143-145), Romanow calls on provincial and territorial governments to begin by "implementing centralized approaches, setting standardized criteria, and providing clear information to patients on how long they can expect to wait." (Ch. 6, p. 138)

> "Taken together, the recommended actions to manage waits lists should achieve three broad goals—fairness, appropriateness, and certainty. Fairness means that wait times are set on objective criteria based on patients' needs rather than by individual providers or hospitals. Appropriateness means that the time people wait is appropriate for their condition. And certainty means that people will have a clear under-

> standing of how long they can expect to wait and why." (Ch. 6, p. 149)

3.3.6 Perennial debate: public vs. private

The Romanow report flags the extent to which the private sector should be involved in health care delivery as "one of the most contentious issues facing Canadians." (Ch. 1, p. 6). He characterizes the debate in the following way:

> "In the face of continuing pressures on the health care system, some argue that more private for-profit service delivery ought to be introduced in order to bring more resources, choice and competition into the Canadian health care system and to improve its efficiency and effectiveness. Others argue as strongly that the private sector should be completely excluded from health care delivery, suggesting that private for-profit delivery runs counter to Canadians' values, is inequitable, and less cost-effective than public delivery in the long run." (Ch. 1, p. 6)

For his part, Romanow strongly endorses public, non-profit delivery of core health care services, and this endorsement underpins the entire report.

> "[T]he Commission believes … that direct health care services should be delivered in public and not-for-profit health care facilities." (Ch. 1, p. 7.)

He takes exception to claims that for-profit delivery is more efficient than not-for-profit delivery.

> "In effect, these [for-profit private] facilities 'cream-off' those services that can be easily and more inexpensively provided on a volume basis, such as cataract surgery or hernia repair. This leaves the public system to provide the more complicated and expensive services from which it is more difficult to control cost per case. But if something goes wrong with a

> patient after discharge from a private facility ... the public system is required to provide a 'back-up' to the private facilities to ensure quality care." (Ch. 1, p. 7)

Moreover, Romanow points to "evidence from the United States to suggest that the non-profit sector tends to have better quality outcomes than the for-profit sector in such things as nursing home care ... and managed care organizations and hospitals." (Ch. 1, p. 7)

Romanow acknowledges that more needs to be done to ensure timely access to quality services. However,

> "[t]he answer ... is not to look to the private sector for solutions. Instead, governments should seek the best solutions within the public system and ensure that adequate resources are available and services are accessible to all." (Ch. 1, p. 8)

Romanow: three areas of specific concern

Having expressed strong support for public, non-profit delivery, the Commission identifies three threatening practices that are currently of concern.

Firstly, Romanow expresses concern about the fact that certain diagnostic services "are provided in private facilities under contracts with regional health authorities or provincial governments." In particular, there is a "growing reliance on the private provision of more advanced and expensive diagnostics such as MRIs (magnetic resonance imaging), for which the waiting times in the public system can be "frustratingly long" because of underinvestment in the public system. According to Romanow, this situation permits "individuals to purchase faster service by paying for these services out of their own pocket and using the test results to 'jump the queue' back into the public system for treatment." Romanow emphasizes that this violates one of the principles of Medicare—that individuals' financial resources should not determine their access to services. Romanow stops short of calling for the elimination of private, for-profit diagnostic service delivery. Instead, he repeats his call for increased public investment in this area so as to remove the temptation for individuals and health care providers "to 'game' the system."[63] Furthermore, he recommends that "diagnostic services be explicitly included under the definition of 'insured health services' under a new *Canada Health Act* (Executive summary, p. xi)." Such a step would curb extra-billing and queue jumping by wealthy individuals.

A second area of concern for Romanow is the preferential treatment received by workers' compensation clients with job-related injuries and illnesses. He reiterates his recommendation that governments "reconsider the current practice by which some workers' compensation agencies contract with private providers to deliver fast-track diagnostic services to potential claimants." (Executive summary, p. xxv)

Thirdly, Romanow decries the contracting out of surgical services such as cataract and some day surgeries. He does not explicitly call for the end of this contracting out; rather he notes that there is no evidence that the practice is more efficient or less costly, and that expanding it could have adverse trade treaty implications. Romanow then re-emphasizes his vision for the existing system:

> "The Commission is strongly of the view that a properly funded public system can continue to provide high quality services to which Canadians have become accustomed. Rather than subsidize private facilities with public dollars, governments should choose to ensure that the public system has sufficient capacity and is universally accessible." (Ch. 1, p. 9)

Significantly, the Romanow report does not extend this logic to many other health-related services, including some that are widely seen as part of the Canada's public health care system.

Romanow's distinction between "direct" and "ancillary" services

In considering the privatization issue, Romanow seeks to distinguish between what he calls "direct health care services such as medical, diagnostic and surgical care" and "ancillary services such as food preparation, cleaning and maintenance." (Ch. 1, p. 6)

In a rather involved passage, Romanow bases the distinction between direct and ancillary services variously on five criteria (Ch. 1, pp. 6-7), namely: complexity; ability to monitor quality; capacity and degree of competition in the private sector; public acceptance; and relative importance. None of these criteria stand up to scrutiny.

- Complexity of delivered services

  "Unlike ancillary services, direct health services are very complex"

This statement misrepresents the nature of the services involved. In fact, there is considerable overlap in their complexity. Some direct health services are fairly simple, while certain ancillary services are quite complex, and vice versa. The critical point, however, is that, taken as a whole, all health care services—surgeries, laundry services, nursing, food services, accounting or administration—are complex to deliver well.

- Ability to monitor quality of contracted service

  "Ancillary services are relative easy to judge in terms of quality—the laundry is either clean or it is not, the cafeteria food is either good or it is not. Consequently, it is relative easy to judge whether the company is providing the service as promised."

  "...[I]t is difficult to assess ... [the] quality [of direct health care services] without considerable expertise. Indeed, the effects of poorly provided service may not be apparent until some time after the service has been delivered, as in the event of a post-operative compli-

> cation. This is what most clearly distinguishes direct health care services from ancillary services…"

Food service and cleaning services are more complex and important than Romanow suggests. Like the effects of poorly provided "direct" health services, the impact of food poisoning or the spread of SARS (see below) "may not be apparent until some time after the service has been delivered." It may, in fact, be quite difficult to assess the quality of these contracted services without considerable expertise. The same can be said for other so-called ancillary health care services such as accounting and hospital administration services.

- Capacity and degree of competition in private sector

With respect to ancillary services, "there is a greater likelihood that there are competitors in the same business to whom hospitals can turn for laundry or food services if their current contractor is unsatisfactory."

For direct health care services, "[i]t is …unlikely that there would be a significant number of competitors able to offer health care services if a given for-profit provider is unsatisfactory. There is simply not a significant surplus of health care administrators or providers waiting in the wings to take over service delivery in a hospital. Thus, if services are of poor quality, it is going to be much harder to find a replacement…"

As U.S. experience shows, expanding for-profit health care in Canada, would greatly increase the number and capacity of for-profit suppliers of direct health care services. This would greatly reduce or eliminate this purported difference between the two types of services. In fact, the limited role of private, for-profit providers in the Canadian health system has been the result of deliberate policy choices, not of any fundamental difference in the nature of direct or so-called ancillary health services.

- Apparent acceptance by the public

> "An increasing proportion of ancillary services provided in Canada's not-for-profit hospitals are now

> contracted out to for-profit corporations. Canadians seem to find this role for private sector companies acceptable..."

The report cites no evidence in support of its implied claim that Canadians would accept contracting out of all health care services that are not deemed to be "direct".

- Relative importance of delivered services

> "[A] poorly prepared cafeteria meal may be unpleasant, but poor quality surgery is another matter altogether."

At the root of Romanow's distinction between direct and ancillary services lies the notion that all direct health care services are intrinsically more important than food services, cleaning services, maintenance services, accounting services, computer and data management services, security services, management services and many other components of the health care system. The recent outbreaks of SARS in Canada and Asia demonstrate the fallacy and danger of this notion. In Taipei, for example, the director of the Center for Disease Control concluded that direct control of nursing aides, cleaners and laundry workers in hospitals should be a key part of preventing the re-emergence of SARS. Near the height of the outbreak, the Taipei Times quoted the director elaborating on this point: "The SARS outbreak has revealed the impropriety of hospitals outsourcing these jobs." At an outbreak in one hospital, for example, "doctors and nurses fortunately were not infected. However, nursing aides, who did not have proper disease-prevention outfits, roamed freely in hospitals and contracted the disease.... These nursing aides, cleaners and laundry workers were not the hospitals' formal employees. The hospitals, therefore could not efficiently manage these workers." In order to improve infection control, the director recommended that all outsourced jobs be brought back under the direct control of hospitals. The Taiwan Health Reform

Foundation's review also cited outsourcing, or contracting out, in its analysis of the flaws in the country's medical system that were exposed by the SARS outbreak.[64]

There is no unambiguous distinction between direct and ancillary health care services. By purporting to draw one using the criteria it does, the Romanow report invites critics to apply the same dubious criteria to direct health care services. While the distinction does not affect the overall logic supporting non-profit delivery, it regrettably colours and weakens the persuasive force of Romanow's main argument. More seriously, the distinction offers tacit approval to privatization and for-profit delivery in a wide range of services that are critical to the health care system. As noted below, both of these results could have important trade treaty implications.

Despite drawing the unwarranted and unfortunate distinction between "direct" and "ancillary" health care services, the Romanow report remains a strong endorsement for public, non-profit health care services generally. Commissioner Romanow reinforced this perspective when he released the report:

> "Forty years ago, when visionary men and women came together to create Medicare, we had private medicine in Canada. You paid out of pocket to receive medical services if you could afford them, or relied on the dole if you couldn't. If you needed an operation, you cashed in your savings, mortgaged your home or sold your farm so you could pay, or you simply did without. If you had the resources or good fortune, you were able to pay you way to the front of the line; if you didn't, you waited and prayed for the best.
>
> Many of the so-called 'new solutions' being proposed for health care—pay-as-you-go, user and facility fees, fast-track treatment for the lucky few, and wait-lists for everyone else—are not new at all. We've been

> there. They are old solutions that didn't work then, and were discarded for that reason. And the preponderance of evidence is that they will not work today.
>
> In the coming months, the choices we make, or the consequences of those we fail to make, will decide Medicare's future. I believe Canadians are prepared to embark on the journey together and build on the proud legacy they have inherited." (Romanow statement, p. 7)

3.3.7 Electronic health records

Like the Mazankowski and Kirby reports, the Romanow report emphasizes the importance of information systems. Deliberately placing information issues near the front of his report, Romanow states that:

> "leading-edge information, technology assessment and research are essential foundations for all of the reforms outlined in subsequent chapters" of his report (Ch. 3, p. 76)

Romanow recommends the establishment of "a personal electronic health record for each Canadian" (Ch. 3, p. 76) as "one of the keys to modernizing Canada's health system and improving access and outcomes for Canadians." (Ch. 3, p. 77) He also recommends an amendment to the Criminal Code to "explicitly prevent the abuse or misuse of personal health information". (Ch. 3, p. 76)

The report endorses the activities of Canada Health Infoway, which it describes as "an independent, non-profit corporation with responsibility for accelerating the development and adoption of modern systems of information technology with the aim of providing better health care." (Ch. 3, p. 79-80). It recommends that the corporation, whose members are the deputy ministers of health across the country, should "continue to take the lead ... for developing a pan-Canadian electronic health record framework built upon provincial systems." (Ch. 3, p. 76) According to Romanow, "Infoway is uniquely poised to provide overall leadership and to act as a catalyst in moving forward on essential information management and technology initiatives." (Ch. 3, p. 80) Significantly, the report merely alludes to the potential for Infoway to obtain private funding, and then, when allowing for this possibility, stating only that it should occur after government "discussion":

> "Further funding, if necessary, should come only after discussion by the federal, provincial and territorial health ministers." (Ch. 3, p. 80)

Elsewhere, however, the prospect for private for-profit involvement is made a little clearer, when the report indicates that health information systems is one of the areas for which public-private partnerships may be acceptable, even given their acknowledged shortcomings:

> "Unfortunately, while P3s may cost governments and taxpayers less in the short term, these arrangements often cost more in the longer term.... The rental costs charged to governments must be high enough to allow the private sector partner to recoup its costs and make a profit for its shareholders. The cost of borrowing is often higher for the private sector than for governments. And P3s often have higher administration costs. Critics also suggest that the quality of private for-profit run facilities can be lower than publicly run facilities and that, in some cases, these arrangements have resulted in beds being closed and staff being reduced... This is not to say that P3s are without a place (for example in the case of health information systems), but they are no panacea and their use and value need to be carefully considered." (Ch. 1, p. 30; italics added)

Despite the importance assigned to health information systems, Romanow's apparent support of public-private partnerships in the sector is not explained, and no evidence is provided that "their use and value [have been] carefully considered." Similarly, even though it claims information systems are one of the "essential foundations" for health care reforms (Ch. 3, p. 76), the report does not examine the trade treaty implications of foreign, for-profit involvement in Canada's health information systems. Such foreign involvement is steadily increasing. Canada Health Infoway, which has a policy of encouraging alliances, partnerships, collaborations and joint investments with the private sector,[65] collaborated in the Alberta Electronic Health Record, the implementation of which was announced in October, 2003 and which "is expected to form the model for provincial health records nation wide."[66] This Infoway-supported project involves the Alberta government and physicians, pharmacists and regional health authorities, as well as Alberta SuperNet (which includes Bell West and Axia SuperNet Limited); and IBM Canada. In May 2004, Canada Health Infoway announced a major partnership arrangement with a U.S.-based corporation to accelerate the development of national electronic health records. (See Section 4.3.3)

3.3.8 Prescription drugs

The Romanow Commission argues that the costs of prescription drugs should eventually be covered under the *Canada Health Act*. The report states:

> "Given the expanding role of prescription drugs in Canada's health care system, a strong case can be made that prescription drugs are just as medically necessary as hospital or physician services... However, the immediate integration of all prescription drugs into a revised *Canada Health Act* has significant implications, not the least of which would be substan-

> tial costs. Therefore, the goal should be to move in a gradual but deliberate and dedicated way to integrate prescription drugs more fully into the continuum of care. Over time, these proposals will raise the floor for prescription drug coverage across Canada and lay the groundwork for the ultimate objective of bringing prescription drugs under the *Canada Health Act*." (Ch. 9, p. 190)

In the near-term, Romanow focuses on reducing financial barriers that prevent some Canadians from accessing the prescription drugs they need and on the continuing need to improve the quality, safety and cost-effectiveness of prescription drugs.

He recommends the establishment of a "Catastrophic Drug Transfer"—additional federal funds "to help cover the high costs of prescription drug plans and protect their residents against the potentially 'catastrophic' impact of high cost drugs." (Ch. 9, p. 190)

He also recommends the establishment of a new National Drug Agency to ensure "the safety, quality and cost-effectiveness of all new drugs before they are approved for use in Canada" (Ch. 9, p. 190) and to review drugs and monitor their use and effectiveness.

All three reports agree that rising prescription drug costs present a significant challenge to the long-term sustainability of the Canadian health care system. According to recent data from the Canadian Institute for Health Information, pharmaceuticals continue to represent the fastest-growing component of health care costs. They accounted for over 15% of total health expenditures in 2001, up from 5.8% of total health spending in 1980.[67] Like the Mazankowski and Kirby reports, Romanow also recommends a national formulary for prescription drugs to "provide consistent coverage, objective assessments, and help contain costs." (Ch. 9, p. 191). Unlike the other reports, Romanow recommends a review of certain aspects of patent protection for prescription drugs.

Romanow asserts that "there is no empirical evidence to suggest that Canada's patent protection laws are responsible for increasing drug prices (emphasis added)" (Ch. 9, p. 209). This terse assertion is quite misleading. Drug prices in Canada are controlled and consequently: "Prices of all drugs, and of patented drugs alone, have continued to remain relatively stable throughout the last half-decade."[68] Nevertheless, there is strong empirical evidence that Canada's patent protection laws are a significant driver of increased spending on drugs.

As the Patent Medicines Price Review Board, the federal government agency charged with regulating drug prices, observed in its most recent report: "In 2001, total sales by drug manufacturers in Canada increased by 15% to $11.5 billion. Patentees reported total factory-gate sales of patented drugs for human use of $7.5 billion. This represents an increase of 18.9% over sales in 2000. Patented drugs now account for 65% of total sales, up from 43.9% in 1995. Increases in sales of drugs have translated to increases in expenditures by public and private drug plans and consumers."[69] Moreover, according to the report, "The rising share of patented drugs within total drug sales may be attributed in part to the long term effects of increased patent protection resulting from Bills C-22 and C-91 in 1987 and 1993."[70] In other words, Canadians are spending more on drugs, at least in part, because of the decreased availability of cheaper generic drugs resulting from changes to Canada's patent protection laws.

Romanow does express concerns about specific practices by the pharmaceutical industry that may have the effect of delaying the development and approval of cheaper generic drugs. The report spotlights the practices of "ever-greening, where manufacturers of brand name drugs make variations to existing drugs in order to extend their patent coverage (Ch. 9, p. 209)" as well as so-called "notice of compliance" regulations that encourage peremptory law suits that delay the introduction of generic alternatives even after the period of monopoly patent protection expires. (Ch. 9, p. 209)" The report also expresses concern about the adverse potential of the patenting of human genes, DNA sequences and cell lines and supports calls for a federal government review of "the current provisions of the patent law in relation to the issues of genes and DNA." (Ch. 9, p. 209)

3.3.9 Globalization and trade treaties

In a marked and commendable departure from the Mazankowski and Kirby reports, the Romanow Commission report examines the potential conflicts between trade treaties and the Canadian health care system. It draws on a variety of sources, including two discussion papers by prominent trade specialists, a public policy dialogue, and a report involving a broad consortium of Canadian academics, researchers and organizations, coordinated by the Canadian Centre for Policy Alternatives.[71]

The Romanow report emphasizes that public concerns about the impact of trade treaties on health care are widespread:

> "In almost every one of the Commission's public hearings as well as the regional roundtables, concerns were expressed by experts and citizens alike that Canada's health care system should be protected from the impact of international trade agreements" (Ch. 11, p. 235).

It also draws attention to the ambiguity of trade treaty protections for public health. For example, in the case of NAFTA annex II social services reservation:

> "there is no clear definition of what constitutes a 'social service' or what determines whether a service is established for a 'public purpose'" (Ch. 11, p. 236).

The report notes that despite the lack of clarity about "what is or what is not protected by the reservation under NAFTA", there is a "strong consensus that the existing single-payer monopoly of Canada's health care system is not subject to a challenge under NAFTA." However, "there is some uncertainty around the question of whether it protects future changes that could be made in the health care system." (Ch. 11, p. 237).

Romanow backs away for making an independent assessment of that uncertainty, stating that "there are no clear and definitive answers to the question of what international trade agreements mean for Canada's health care system." (Ch. 11, p. 238). However, he indicates that trade treaties should not stifle change but recommends policymakers adopt an assertive approach:

> "Rather than conclude ... that Canada is hemmed in to the current system and cannot change, the more reasonable conclusion is that if we want to expand the range of services in the public system, it is better to do it now while there still is very little foreign presence in health care in Canada and the potential costs of [trade] compensation are low." (Ch. 11, p. 238).[72]

Overall, Romanow highlights the importance of protecting the health care system from trade treaty challenges, recommending it as one of the three key "Directions for Change" in Health Care and Globalization. (Ch. 11, p. 233) The report emphasizes the need for:

> "[s]teps will be taken here in Canada and on the world stage to preserve and protect Canada's publicly funded health care system against any potential challenges under international trade agreements." (Ch. 11, p. 246)

Romanow also proposes that health care imperatives should take precedence over free trade rules. Canada should

> "work with other countries, especially those in the World Trade Organization, to ensure that when it comes to important social policy areas such as health

> cares, all countries have the right to chart their own course independent of international trade agreements." (Ch. 11, p. 246)

3.4 The Courchene paper

In October 2003, the Institute for Research on Public Policy published a short paper on the Kirby and Romanow reports by Queens University Economics Professor Thomas Courchene. Courchene's paper helps to dramatize some of the fundamental differences between the Kirby and Romanow approaches to health care reform. The paper also provides insight into the hostility with which some proponents of private, for-profit health care, including Courchene himself, view Canada's existing Medicare system.

Courchene's main argument is that the underlying principles contained in Romanow report cannot provide for the "successful evolution" of the health care system, whereas those in the Kirby report can. This analysis is deeply coloured by Courchene's "admittedly subjective view of the likely evolution of Canada's health care system in the information era (p. 8)." Indeed, he merely defines "success" as being in accord with his particular vision of the future. In doing so, the paper confuses prescriptive with prospective, suggesting that only recommendations that reinforce current trends toward health care commercialization are viable.

3.4.1 Courchene's analysis of the Romanow report

According to Courchene, the Canadian values or operating principles outlined in the Romanow report

> "fall well short of a blueprint for ensuring the successful evolution of Canada's health care system in the information era." (p. 8)

> "These values / principles / instruments will not ... ensure the viability of Canada's health care system in the 21st century." (p. 11)

The Romanow report's "operating principles ... do not square well with the manner in which the health sector is evolving in the 21st century." (p. 14)

By contrast, according to Courchene, the "corresponding operating principles underpinning the Kirby report are more incentive-compatible (sic) with the dictates and the dynamism of the information era." (p. 19)

Relying on a single sub-section of the Commissioner's introduction to the final report, Courchene professes to distil the essence of the Romanow report down to four "operating principles" or "Canadian values" that, Courchene asserts, Romanow deems "integral to Canada's medicare system."

These Canadian values (or CV1-4 as Courchene prefers) are:

- "CV-1 Medicare is a moral enterprise"
- "CV-2 Prohibition of private money"
- "CV-3 Co-opt private diagnostic providers; discourage if not prohibit private treatment providers," and
- "CV-4: "Canada has latched on to the best approach to health care so that experimentation with alternative approaches can be discouraged."[73]

After crudely reformulating the "essence" of the Romanow report in this manner, Courchene then unfavourably contrasts these imputed "values" to his own personal vision of the future of health care in the 21st century.

For Courchene, the growth of private, for-profit health care is a key aspect of "success" in the future. This trend, he suggests, is inevitable:

> "[T]he future on the health front will be characterized by a rapid growth of innovative and specialized diagnostic and treatment centres that will be separate

> from, although possibly aligned with, the hospital sector.... [T]hese specialized clinics will in all likelihood be privately owned and operated. The policy issue here is not whether they should be allowed to proliferate, but rather how they ought to be integrated with Canada's health care system." (pp. 12-13)

Courchene correctly states that

> "[T]he public-private integrated vision ... of 21st century health care runs directly counter to the letter and even more so to the spirit of the Romanow Report's 'system based on Canadian values.'" (p. 13)

As noted, Courchene criticizes Romanow for pointing out, quite accurately, that the majority of "Canadians view medicare as a moral enterprise, not a business venture (Courchene, p. 9; Romanow, p. xx). Courchene's retort is worrisome. On the one hand, he argues that health care must be seen as "both an essential social institution and a dynamic economic sector for production, exports and employment." (p. 12) On the other hand, however, he goes further, stating:

> "the reality is that in an information era the health care sector will need a massive infusion of physical, intellectual and financial capital to enable it to become a dynamic engine of economic growth... Viewing the health sector solely as a social policy endeavour will almost surely guarantee that it will never receive this requisite infusion..." (italics in original)

Also,

> "If viability in the information era means that the health care sector must transcend the social sphere, it is a fortiori the case that it must also transcend the vision of medicare as a 'moral enterprise.'" (underlining added)

Courchene's position is thus laid bare. He discounts the potential for a significant "infusion of physical, intellectual and financial capital" into the existing health care system. Moreover, he evidently believes that Canada's health care sector must in future transcend—be above or independent of—the social sphere ... and above, or independent of, moral concerns. Even allowing for an economist's bias, this view is disconcertingly extreme.

Courchene goes on to castigate Romanow for supporting measures that prevent wealthy individuals from purchasing privileged access to covered publicly insured heath services and preclude private insurers from insuring services covered by Medicare (CV-2). Courchene does so without ever clearly acknowledging that this prohibition defines Medicare's public health insurance monopoly or that such practices would clearly contravene the *Canada Health Act*.

Courchene's portrayal of Romanow as rejecting experimentation with alternative approaches (CV-4) is risible. Obviously, the Romanow report contains many recommendations for reforming and renewing the Canadian health care system. The Romanow report in no way turns its back on experimentation. It simply, after consideration of the evidence presented to it, rejects Courchene's preferred "radical solutions" such as "user fees, medical savings accounts, de-listing services, greater privatization, [and] a parallel private system" (Romanow, p. xx, cited in Courchene, p. 11).

3.4.2 Courchene's analysis of the Kirby report

The most valuable aspects of the Courchene paper are the insights it provides into the aims and effects of health care commercialization proposed in the Kirby report. Overall, Courchene concludes that "the Kirby Report model [would tilt] the evolution of Canada's health care system in the direction of becoming a leading sector for employment, research, innovation and exports." But Courchene makes other notable points about the Kirby report.

Kirby's health care guarantee: promoting for-profit delivery; towards a two-tier health care system

Courchene notes that together a health care guarantee and the "competitive provision of insured services" would constitute "fundamental departures from the status quo...." The latter would constitute, alternatively, "a reinterpretation" (p. 15) or

> "a creative (and information-era-compatible) interpretation" (p. 16) of the public administration principle of the *Canada Health Act*.

He acknowledges that

> "Of and by itself, the [Kirby] health care guarantee could prove to be very expensive indeed..." (p. 16)

Courchene also alludes to the coercive nature of the proposed health care guarantee, where the potential expense of foreign treatment would spur increases in private, for-profit delivery of diagnostic and treatment services within Canada's publicly funded health care system:

> "Allowing competitive provision of diagnostic and treatment services is absolutely essential to the working of the Kirby Report's health care guarantee, if for no other reason than domestic private provision is for a variety of reasons ... likely to be considerably less expensive than resorting to treatment in the US." (p. 18)

In fact, according to Courchene, this proposal could lead to the development of a genuine two-tier health care system.

> "[T]he requirement in the Kirby Report model for a 'residual supplier' to accommodate the demand arising from breaching a health care guarantee may well ensure that some version of a parallel private system will develop." (p. 18-9)

Kirby effects: Reduced wages and benefits for health care workers, fewer public sector workers

Courchene's paper indicates that the purported cost-effectiveness of private diagnostic and treatment centres would depend in part upon "greater flexibility in terms of employment relations and professional practices." (p. 12-3) This claim is later repeated:

> "The deliberate introduction of competition between public and private service providers within the publicly funded system "will generate important cost savings" in part because of "more flexible employment relations [and] ... more flexible professional practices/ procedures..." (p. 18)

Courchene quotes Kirby elaborating on this point in a speech that he delivered in May, 2003:

> "Moving toward service-based funding will eliminate much, if not all, of [the]wrangling [between health care institutions and governments] since the government will no longer be involved in the micro-management of hospital budgets. Amongst other things, this could contribute to a significant downsizing of provincial health care bureaucracies." (p. 17)

In other passages of the same speech (which Courchene does not quote), Kirby makes the point more broadly:

> "[S]trengthening the role of the regional health authority—the 'middleman'—would effectively break up the existing supply-side monopoly and allow for greater supply-side competition within the publicly funded health-care system."
>
> "Health care, as it is presently structured, has given certain groups excessive, indeed virtual monopoly, power over the delivery of what is, after all, an essential service, health care."

Ultimately, the most valuable aspect of Courchene's paper may be how it elucidates some of the impacts that would result from the Kirby report's recommendations to fundamentally restructure the Canadian health care system. Probing beneath Kirby's carefully worded recommendations, Courchene recognises a fellow-traveller, who by creating "internal markets at the core of its design and delivery mechanism, means that the Canadian health care system would have the ability to evolve from within (p. 19, emphasis in the original)" to fit Courchene's own harsh vision of 21st century Canadian heath care.

CHAPTER 4

Hazardous mixture: trade treaties and health care reform proposals

4.1 At odds: Trade treaty principles and Medicare principles

MODERN TRADE TREATIES ARE BASED ON the promotion of freer flows of goods, services and investments, which is achieved primarily by constraining and re-directing the regulatory ability of governments. By contrast, Canada's health care system is designed to provide health care services to all citizens on the basis of need rather than the ability to pay, which is achieved by deliberately constraining and, in certain instances, prohibiting the operation of market forces. These two principles—one primarily commercial, the other public—are at odds. Moreover, the potential for discord between the two is growing as governments expand the scope of trade treaties and increasingly commercialize health care services.

Far too often, this rising conflict between free trade and health care priorities escapes public scrutiny. Sometimes, as in the case of the Mazankowski and Kirby reports, the conflict is not considered and its practical significance to health care reform never discussed. In general, the issue receives diverse treatment. For instance, the conflict may sometimes remain unrecognized, or be misconstrued. Some observers may mistakenly assume that public health and trade policy are fully compatible. Others may incorrectly presume that health care policies are beyond the reach of trade treaties. Still others may focus attention almost exclusively on the perceived importance of global commercial interests, and play down the significance of citizens' public health priorities. Some analysts appear to confuse the process of increased global economic integration with the particular kinds of rules that are found in modern trade treaties, as if the international legal norms that shape globalization were beyond debate. And others, perhaps unconsciously, may fatalistically assume that the current generation of trade treaty rules will inevitably supercede other social priorities, no matter how critical those priorities may be.

In assessing proposals for health care reform in Canada, it is necessary to consider the underlying clash of principles and to analyze its practical effects. Which types of health care proposals would most expose citizens and their governments to challenge under trade treaty rules? Which approaches would minimize the risk of these trade treaty challenges? What changes to trade treaty obligations and negotiating objectives are needed to avoid future conflict? Of what other practical significance is the growing conflict between trade treaty rules and health care reform, now and in the future?

4.2 Flashpoints in the health care reports

There are a number of recommendations contained in the three health care reports that, if implemented, would constitute areas of particular conflict—"flashpoints"—between trade treaty rules and public health care imperatives. All of the reports contain some recommendations that would increase the likelihood of future trade challenges. However, the Romanow report stands in stark contrast to the others; it is the only report to have examined the trade issue, and implementing its most important recommendations would generally reduce trade treaty vulnerabilities now and in the future. The Mazankowski and Kirby reports, on the other hand, both recommend changes that would sharply increase the risk of trade challenges.

Overall, increased involvement by foreign corporations in the Canadian health care system increases the potential for, and vulnerability to, challenges under trade treaty rules. This development, if left unchecked, poses one of the greatest risks to Medicare and to the success of future health care reform in Canada.

4.2.1. Public-private partnerships (P3s)

Commercializing health care is a key theme of the Mazankowski and Kirby reports. As discussed above, implementing their recommendations would entail a significant expansion of private, for-profit health care delivery. Curiously, despite the attention that public-private partnership proposals have attracted in recent years, neither report dwells on them. No concerns are raised about these types of arrangements, and both reports provide implicit support for the concept. For example, the Mazankowski discussion of regional "care groups, " while not advocating public-private partnerships specifically, could readily conform to, and is strongly suggestive of, a joint public-private arrangement for facilities and an intermingling of public and private, for-profit service delivery. So too is that report's proposal for the various aspects of the health care system to be "unbundled." Similarly, Kirby promotes devolving authority to regional authorities and increasing competition in health care—both of which imply a supportive environment for public-private arrangements.

The Romanow report raises important concerns about public-private partnerships. He notes that they "often cost more in the longer term"—due to higher rental costs, higher cost of borrowing, and higher administration costs—and have been criticized for providing lower-quality services. He concludes that P3s "are no panacea and their use and value need to be carefully considered." (p. 30)

A public-private partnership can be defined as an arrangement between the public and private sector for the purpose of delivering a project or a service that is traditionally provided by the public sector. There are many models of P3s, and the degree of private sector involvement may vary widely. At one end of the spectrum, for example, public assets may be privatized, or turned over to the private sector. Similarly, services traditionally delivered by public employees may be contracted out for delivery by private, for-profit corporations. Other arrangements involve the private sector in operating and maintaining publicly-owned facilities; designing, building, financing and operating new facilities under long-term leases; or financing, building owning and operating a facility or providing a service for a specified time or in perpetuity. All of these arrangements involve differing degrees of accountability, control and financial risk.[74]

P3s in health infrastructure

The Romanow report appears to offer support for public-private partnerships in health information systems but, as indicated above, this support is limited and the reference somewhat oblique. The Mazankowski report is more explicit, recommending governments and health authorities consider P3s as one of the alternatives to developing or purchasing the information technology that would be necessary for electronic health care cards. Kirby clearly supports a public-private partnership in information technology, which in the report is considered a key aspect of health care infrastructure. In particular, the Kirby report focuses on developing a national system of electronic health records. This proposal has been advanced by a private, not-for-profit corporation, known as Canada Health Infoway Inc, whose corporate members are deputy ministers of health, and whose board of directors have diverse (often private health industry or information technology) backgrounds. The Kirby committee underlines its enthusiasm for the corporation's work, and recommends that the federal government provide it additional financial support. In addition to this increased federal funding, Kirby asserts that an electronic health record system would "require ... partnerships with the private sector".

The new federal Liberal administration under Prime Minister Paul Martin provided $100 million to Canada Health Infoway in March 2004, and Infoway subsequently announced an arrangement with Chicago-based Initiate Systems, Inc. "aimed at accelerating the development of Canada-wide electronic health records." (See Section 4.3.3)

Public-private partnerships raise important health policy concerns. Four prominent economists and a former director of audit operations with Canada's Auditor General recently characterized P3 hospitals as "a serious threat to the public health care system."[75] In their crisp analysis, the authors criticize P3 hospitals on the basis of increased cost, diminished public accountability, and a deterioration of the quality and extent of universal service. They conclude:

> "When properly accounted for, it is clear that public ownership and not-for-profit administration will cost provincial taxpayers less, and result in hospitals that more clearly operate in the interests of patients and in accordance with the requirements and criteria of the *Canada Health Act*."

The involvement, including through various forms of P3s, of private, for-profit corporations in health care administration and information management raises other important concerns about privacy and democratic accountability.[76] Despite these concerns, contracting out health information systems is increasingly common, and many for-profit corporations anticipate hefty profits.

According to a recent article in the Financial Times of London,[77]

> "In the UK, the National Health Service has just signed 10-year contracts worth more than £5.5bn to provide electronic patient records, e-booking, e-prescribing and electronic ordering of tests, in what is arguably the world's biggest civil [information technology] procurement—one that will cover all 50m patients in England and 1m staff. The programme should also see digital images replace x-ray film, making consultation on a patient's condition possible remotely."
>
> "Computer giants such as International Business Machines [IBM], SAP, Hewlett-Packard and Dell, and niche software specialists such as Cerner of Kansas City and Eclipsis of Florida, all want a share of what is expected to be a very large market. 'This is the next big thing,' says Tom McCausland, president and CEO of the US division of Siemens Medical Systems, a leader in healthcare technology."
>
> "'We are looking at an area where you will find about 10-20 per cent growth,' estimates Neil de Crescenzo,

healthcare industry leader at IBM Business Consulting Services. 'What we have seen so far is just the beginning.'"

Critically, for the purposes of this book, P3s—not just in information technology but in other health areas—raise serious trade treaty problems.

Since public-private partnerships are a specific form of health care commercialization, P3s suffer from most of the trade problems that have already been considered. Because they can span almost the entire range of health care services, P3s represent the potential for foreign corporations to use trade policy rules to distort key aspects of Canadian health care policy.

For example, under domestic laws, governments must satisfy rigorous legal requirements that protect the rights of both parties whenever they cancel contracts with private service providers for inadequate service or other legitimate public reasons. Trade treaty rules, particularly NAFTA investment provisions, are biased towards the rights of the foreign investor, requiring governments to provide affected foreign corporations financial compensation for measures that are broadly defined as expropriation. P3s could encompass most health sectors, including information systems, hospital construction, hospital ownership and investment, the ownership and investment of other health care facilities and other infrastructure, and even the management and day-to-day operation of health care facilities and entire systems. In each of these areas, to the extent that P3s would entail increased involvement by foreign corporations, trade rules make canceling these arrangements more expensive and difficult than would otherwise be the case. Trade treaties therefore shift much of the risk of failed P3s to governments, in effect insuring the private partners at taxpayer expense.

P3s in areas covered by trade treaty rules would also constrain governments' ability to maximize local, regional or national benefits, or achieve other social goals, for example, by favouring domestic non-profit providers, negotiating performance requirements, or enforcing quantity-based quotas and restrictions. All of these conditions, which in theory can be written into P3 agreements to make them more palatable, are disallowed by trade and investment treaty rules.

Finally, where governments choose to contract for services (rather than providing them directly) adopting a traditional procurement model—where governments purchase and pay for the required services directly—usually provides the greatest clarity and protection under trade treaties. For example, Canadian provincial and local government procurement is not covered under the NAFTA or the WTO Agreement on Government Procurement. Structuring a service contract as a procurement therefore minimizes trade treaty entanglement. But most P3s do not follow a standard procurement model. Consequently, there are strong arguments that they are subject to the investment and services, rather than the procurement, rules of the NAFTA and the GATS. This greatly increases the risk of trade treaty challenge and of governments facing fines or trade sanctions for the breach of trade treaties with regard to the operation, management or termination of a P3.

Under trade treaties, P3s thus have the potential to diminish governments' regulatory ability in vital areas of health care policy, to shift risk from the investor or service provider to the public, and to increase costs through trade fines or sanctions.

4.2.2 Reducing the scope of public insurance coverage

The Mazankowski approach would almost certainly lead to the expansion of private health care insurance and a retrenchment of the existing public insurance system. Under the Mazankowski recommendations, the list of publicly-insured health care services would either be frozen at its current level or reduced. An expert panel would determine what services should be removed from the public insurance system.[78] Moreover, the Mazankowski approach to public insurance coverage for most new treatments, services or drugs would preclude an expansion of the public insurance system. New services would be covered only if there were sufficient existing revenues to cover the costs or if other services were removed from the list of publicly-covered services. The report explicitly envisions the removal of services and treatments from the list of publicly-insured services, noting that citizens would pay for these privately, in part through private supplementary insurance.

This approach would have a number of trade treaty implications.

Firstly, any reductions in public health insurance coverage would be difficult and expensive for future governments to reverse. The Government of Canada has listed health insurance as one of its GATS specific commitments, and GATS National Treatment and Market Access rules therefore apply in this sector.[79] As a result, bringing de-listed services back within the universe of publicly-insured services could cause foreign service providers whose commercial opportunities are adversely affected to pressure their home government to mount trade challenges against Canada.

Individual foreign investors could also be expected to use NAFTA's controversial investor-to-state dispute settlement process to mount direct challenges against re-insuring health care services under the public insurance system. These investors could seek financial payments as compensation for what under NAFTA rules is broadly considered expropriation of their for-profit insurance business.

Secondly, de-listing health care services from the universe of publicly-insured services would make it more difficult to regulate aspects of privately-insured services within Canada. Canada's existing GATS commitments in Market Access mean that Canadian governments are precluded from limiting the numbers of insurance suppliers for these services, for example, or the number of offices a foreign supplier is permitted to have in any region, or limits on the involvement of foreign investors. Canada's National Treatment commitments, which apply to subsidies, would also prevent the possibility of targeting subsidies to domestic insurance co-operatives, non-profit insurers, or domestic for-profit insurance suppliers of the de-listed services.

Thirdly, shrinking the universe of publicly-insured services would reduce the effectiveness of existing protections against certain trade treaty rules. For example, NAFTA's social services exclusion (Annex II-C-9) provides only limited protection. It allows Canadian governments to adopt or maintain otherwise-inconsistent health care measures only to the extent that they are "social services established or maintained for a public purpose". As noted in the CCPA consortium report,[80] there is sharp disagreement about the scope and efficacy of this safeguard. However, while the protection that the II-C-9 exclusion now affords remains unclear, its ability to shield Canadian health care measures from NAFTA rules would be diminished by the Mazankowski proposals. Reductions in the number and scope of publicly-insured services would shrink the universe of health care services that are protected by virtue of them being "established or maintained for a public purpose."

Finally, it should be noted that Canada's GATS commitments undeniably apply to private health insurance. Canada has listed "life, accident and health insurance services" as covered services in its GATS schedule.[81] This means that foreign health insurers are guaranteed full access to the Canadian private insurance market and to any advantages, including subsidies, provided to Canadian private insurers. It also means that if Canada expands its public health insurance system, that it is required by the GATS to compensate other WTO members for their lost market access.[82] This compensation takes the form or "adjustments" in Canada's schedule (not monetary compensation as under the NAFTA investor-state dispute system), but if adjustments cannot be successfully negotiated, then Canada could face trade sanctions from other WTO member governments. Obviously, the greater the degree of foreign penetration of the Canadian health insurance market, the higher the level of compensation or sanctions that Canadians could ultimately face.[83]

4.2.3 Expanding private for-profit delivery of publicly-insured services

For the Mazankowski commission, contracting public insurance coverage would be only the first step in restructuring the Canadian health care system. Mazankowski also proposes sharp increases in private delivery of those health care services that remain within the public insurance system. Instead of providing health services, governments' primary role would be reduced to setting health policy and allocating funding. Regional health authorities would deliver or contract with private, for-profit and private, non-profit corporations and agencies for the delivery of a full range of publicly-insured services. The Mazankowski approach would open the door to for-profit foreign companies or their affiliates to become directly involved in most or all publicly-insured health care services.

The Kirby report also proposes diminishing government's role to system governance, policy setting and funding, with a new focus on market-based devolution of authority. The report recommends funding be service-based largely because this would allow the government, as funder, to be neutral on the issue of whether health-care institutions are publicly owned or owned by private not-for-profit or for-profit organizations. Though the report does not emphasize the point, it is significant that service-based funding would also be neutral on the issue of whether services are publicly delivered or contracted out to private—including foreign—service suppliers.

Kirby explicitly promotes increased private delivery of some publicly-insured services, including day surgery and long term care, on the basis that this would enhance competition with public service providers.

In accordance with the report's theme of increased competition, it is noteworthy that Kirby's proposal to expand public insurance to include home care envisions private delivery. The expansion of the scope of public insurance coverage would thus come at the cost of consolidating and facilitating private, for-profit delivery—including by foreign affiliated suppliers—in the new publicly-insured services.

The Romanow report advocates strongly for public, non-profit delivery of core health care services, and expresses concerns about increases in the private delivery of publicly-insured services including certain diagnostic and surgical services. Romanow's position is based on his underlying vision of the health care system providing timely access to quality health care services as a right of citizenship. However, the report also notes that public, non-profit delivery has the added benefit of reducing the risks of successful trade treaty challenges. As noted above, the Romanow report draws a distinction between "direct" and "ancillary" health care services. In doing so, the report lends tacit approval to increased privatization, commercialization and for-profit delivery—presumably including by foreign suppliers—of a significant range of important health care services. As noted in Chapter 3, these services could include food services, cleaning services, laundry services, maintenance services, accounting services, computer and data management services, security services, accounting services, management services and many other components of the health care delivery system that are vital for high-quality health care.

Expanding for-profit service delivery, which would increase the degree of foreign involvement in the Canadian health care system, would have several important trade treaty implications.

Increased for-profit health care delivery reduces the effectiveness of existing, and future, protections for health care under current trade treaties.

The NAFTA Annex I general reservation permits provincial, territorial and local governments to maintain existing health care measures that do not conform to certain NAFTA rules. The treaty only permits changes to those measures that increase their conformity with NAFTA rules. Once such a provincial non-conforming measure—ensuring non-profit delivery of diagnostic lab services or cataract operations, for example—is changed so as to be more NAFTA consistent, protection for the original measure is lost forever. Increased commercialization thus permanently reduces the number and types of existing health measures that remain protected from the full force of the treaty.

As noted above, NAFTA Annex II-C-9 provides protection for future government measures against certain NAFTA obligations. This Annex protects otherwise NAFTA inconsistent health measures that are deemed to be "social services established or maintained for a public purpose." Some analysts maintain that this safeguard is sufficiently broad to protect services that are publicly-funded, whether they are delivered publicly or privately. Others assert that the Annex protects publicly-insured services. Still other analysts have expressed concerns that this crucial reservation may be interpreted narrowly, exposing health care measures that disadvantage foreign private interests to successful challenge under NAFTA rules.[84]

Despite the wide range of views about the efficacy of the protective annex, several observations can be made with confidence. It is clear that the scope of this protective provision remains undefined, untested and controversial. Also, critically, increasing private delivery of publicly-insured services shifts the character of such services along the spectrum from those provided for a "public purpose" towards those provided for a "private purpose," which are fully subject to applicable NAFTA rules. Finally, it must be acknowledged that in the event of a dispute, the scope of the Annex in any particular case will ultimately be determined not by governments but by appointed NAFTA arbitral panelists.

Increasing private delivery of publicly-insured services could also reduce the effectiveness of parallel protections in the GATS. The key GATS "governmental authority" exclusion purportedly protects measures pertaining to services "supplied in the exercise of governmental authority." But this protection applies only to services that are provided neither on a commercial nor a competitive basis. Increasing private delivery of publicly-insured services, arguably opening the services to commercialism or competition, would thus make it far more difficult, if not impossible, for governments to satisfy these criteria. Specifically, even services that continue to be provided publicly on a non-commercial basis, may be deemed to be "in competition with" a newly-commercialized "like" service. In this indirect way, commercialization could lead to the loss by publicly-delivered services of any protection the "governmental authority" would otherwise have afforded. The proliferation of private health care delivery could thus greatly increase the number and types of health care services falling within the scope of the GATS.

Increasing for-profit health care would increase foreign corporations' stake and influence in the Canadian health care system and trade policy-making.

As the number of for-profit health service suppliers increases, so too would foreign, for-profit service providers, of which most would be large transnational corporations. Many of these new entrants into the Canadian system would likely be U.S.-based and have longer experience in for-profit health care, deeper pockets and other "comparative advantages" over their Canadian for-profit counterparts and, especially, Canadian not-for-profit health service providers. They would also gain influence as "stakeholders" in Canadian health policy-making and, of direct relevance to this analysis, in health-related trade policy.

Trade treaty rules make reversing increases in for-profit health care delivery much more difficult and expensive.

Under the NAFTA, U.S. investors and service suppliers would acquire certain investment rights that are not enjoyed by Canadian investors or service suppliers. In particular, if future Canadian governments took steps to reverse health care commercialization by returning services to the public or not-for-profit sector, U.S. investors could mount investor-to-state challenges, claiming financial compensation for what they would assert, using the NAFTA definition, to be expropriation. Even if the Canadian measures were non-discriminatory, treating Canadian and American firms alike, the Canadian government would still face an increased risk of compensation claims. The increased complexity and financial liability caused by NAFTA investment rules would thus make it far more difficult and expensive to reverse health care commercialization.

Similarly, under the GATS, any health-related services that a future Canadian government decided to subject to the treaty's national treatment and market access rules would entitle foreign providers to receive the same subsidies as their Canadian counterparts. Subsequently retracting such a benefit from foreign firms could cause the companies' home governments to mount GATS challenges to such discriminatory treatment. To reiterate, the more involved foreign investors and service providers become in the health care system the more difficult and costly it will be, in future, to limit or reverse the trend toward commercialization — no matter how pressing or legitimate the underlying public policy purpose.

4.2.4. Expanding private for-profit delivery of services that are not publicly-insured

The Mazankowski report proposes moving away from public funding towards a system that relies more on private funding for privately-delivered services. It forcefully recommends "diversifying" health care funding sources away from general taxation—that is, away from the single, publicly funded health insurance system. As noted above, the report recommends breaking up what it terms a "public monopoly" in favour of greater private sector involvement and private sources of funding. The latter would not be limited to user fees, variable premiums, new health care taxes and medical savings accounts, but would extend to allowing privately funded and delivered health services and expanding private supplementary health insurance coverage and indeed "private insurance." The report does not rule out, but rather appears to favour, "a privately funded and privately delivered health care system [which] provide[s] the most choice."

The Kirby report generally avoids considering the issue of privately funded and delivered services. Instead, it emphasizes the importance of public funding to be provided without regard for whether services are publicly or privately delivered.

The Romanow report repeatedly emphasizes the fundamental importance of publicly-delivered, not-for-profit health care facilities and "direct" health care, but leaves the door open for private delivery and insurance for other health-related services.

The expansion of privately funded and delivered health services, and the increased foreign involvement that would result, would have several trade implications.

As noted above, trade treaty rules make it far more challenging for governments to bring or return private health care services involving foreign suppliers within the public sphere. For example, expanding the public insurance system to cover post-acute home care services as recommended by Kirby and

Romanow, would be rendered more complicated by a rapid spread of U.S.-based corporations involved in supplying or administering these services. The heightened threat of NAFTA-based compensation cases could also frustrate Canadian government efforts to ensure that these services were publicly-provided, or supplied on a not-for-profit basis. The more foreign corporations become involved in a proliferation of private health care services, the more difficult and expensive these types of initiatives would become, no matter how urgent and legitimate the public need.

The proliferation of privately delivered and funded services with foreign involvement could also reduce the scope of existing and future trade treaty protections for health care. These services would almost certainly lie outside the scope of the protection afforded by NAFTA Annex II-C-9, as arbitral panels would likely reject claims that they were "social services established or maintained for a public [as opposed to a private] purpose." Thus, in these service sectors, NAFTA grants foreign investors the right to mount investor-to-state challenges to demand compensation for harm allegedly caused by Canadian government measures affecting these service sectors. Increased private, for-profit health care in Canada paves the way for increased involvement of U.S. or Mexican corporations and investors. NAFTA's investment provisions consolidate this process, effectively rendering such increasing foreign presence in the Canadian health care system almost a "one-way" street.

Under the GATS, the spread of privately funded, privately delivered health-related services—whether or not they were previously publicly-insured—could result in an unanticipated expansion of the reach of the WTO services treaty. Such services, which are clearly "commercial," would obviously not reside within the purported safety of the GATS "governmental authority" exclusion and so would be subject to all applicable GATS rules. But there is a more subtle and ominous effect of commercialization. It is well understood that commercial health care services are by definition unprotected by the exclusion. However, certain non-commercial public services may also be unprotected. Wherever public, non-commercial services are deemed to be "in competition with" those commercialized for-profit services, these publicly-supplied services cease to be shielded by the GATS "governmental authority" exclusion. The exclusion does not apply to services that are provided "in competition with one or more service suppliers."[85] Thus even services that continue to be publicly-delivered on a non-commercial basis could lose their excluded status merely as a result of being deemed to be in competition with a commercial service. In other words, commercializing health care services could drag related public, non-commercial services out of the protective governmental authority "lifeboat" where these services may otherwise have remained safe from GATS rules.[86] Thus, increasing private, foreign-affiliated, for-profit health care has the potential to indirectly extend the reach of the GATS even deeper into the heart of the Canadian health care system.[87]

4.2.5. More private for-profit health care delivery: Market-based devolution; health care guarantee; care groups

Both the Mazankowski and Kirby reports contain recommendations that would increase the role of private health care delivery in a variety of ways, and that would likely entail increased involvement of foreign for-profit providers in Canada's health care system. As we have seen, it is this foreign involvement that has particularly significant trade treaty implications.

Devolving health care decision-making to regional authorities is a central theme of the Mazankowski and Kirby reports.

Mazankowski proposes that regional health authorities be allowed to contract out many health services, including primary health care, to physicians, labs, private surgical facilities, clinics, and groups of health care providers that operate on either a not-for-profit or for-profit basis. While

Mazankowski suggests that most of these contracted privately-delivered services would be publicly funded, the report does not rule out privately-funded, privately delivered services. As noted above, implementing these recommendations would open the door to foreign, for-profit corporations, established as what Mazankowski calls "care groups," becoming directly involved in nearly all aspects of the health care system.

For Kirby, devolution is linked to service-based funding and the introduction of "internal markets." While more oblique than the Mazankowski report, the Kirby recommendations would also open the door to increased involvement by foreign, for-profit corporations operating in Canada or offering cross-border health care services from the U.S. or elsewhere.

Foreign involvement in Canada's health care system would also increase as a result of the proposal, contained in both reports, of a health care guarantee. Those individuals who did not receive treatment within a specified time would obtain treatment in another region, province or country and the costs would be charged to the patient's home region. Foreign-based providers—especially those based in the U.S.—would be direct beneficiaries of this system, and could initially expect increasing business. Perversely, meeting the increased costs of U.S. service providers would make it even more difficult for cash-strapped regional authorities to meet the guarantee and more likely to face paying for foreign-supplied services in the future.

In each of these cases, the growth in foreign involvement, coupled with the NAFTA and GATS obligations noted above, would make the underlying policies of commercialization far more difficult to reverse.

However, the implications are even broader. As Courchene astutely implies, the high-cost-for-foreign-services dilemma would likely trigger the expansion of private, for-profit delivery of diagnostic and treatment services within Canada, because this would be much less expensive than resorting to treatment in the U.S.. Once again, however, this development would entail increased involvement by foreign-affiliated service corporations operating in Canada and foreign investors in domestic "residual suppliers" of health services. Such private health care suppliers operating on a for-profit basis would almost certainly fall outside the protection of the NAFTA health care reservations, entitling US corporations to establish in Canada and requiring governments to accord them non-discriminatory treatment.[88]

Both the Mazankowski and Kirby reports point to the increasing potential for two-tier health care—private insurance for privately-delivered services—in Canada. As previously noted, Kirby claims to "passionately hope" that such a parallel system will not develop as a result of a court challenge.[89] At the same time, however, his committee's recommendations would increase pressure for the development of just such a system. More directly, the Mazankowski report suggests that private "supplementary" health insurance could provide one way for individuals to compensate for a decreasing scope of public health insurance coverage. Such a two-tier health care system would, of course, entail a steady encroachment by U.S. and other foreign for-profit insurance firms and service providers into the very heart of the Canadian health care system. Yet again, applicable NAFTA and GATS rules would render this growing foreign intrusion very difficult and expensive to reverse.

4.2.6. Telehealth

All three reports hail the positive impact that recent technological advancements could have on health-related information systems or in providing certain services in remote communities. These developments are unquestionably significant — not least because they offer the potential to overcome some of the many challenges that the nation's huge land area pose to the health care system, such as servicing remote communities. However, the reports' apparent faith, for example, that the development of electronic health records will be a major factor in improving the health care status of citizens seems misplaced, bordering on naïve or even disingenuous.[90] Also, none of the reports examine how such technological developments can complicate, or impair, governments' ability to regulate in the health care area. Significantly, from the standpoint of this study, neither do the reports consider the potential trade implications of such technology-driven developments. For example, telecommunications advances provide the opportunity for:

- specialists to interpret x-rays, ultrasound, echo cardiogram and other diagnostic tests remotely;
- specialized organizations to provide on-line education and training to prospective health care workers at all levels;
- doctors and other health care professionals to provide one-on-one consultations by telephone or video link;
- distant computer and information service providers to maintain, store, manage, analyze and market data and information concerning patients' health records, treatment efficacy, and facilities' financial records.

A growing number of vital aspects of the Canadian health care system can be delivered remotely and, significantly, could be obtained from U.S. or other foreign, for-profit corporations. Under trade treaty rules, these electronic services are likely to be seen as equivalent, or "like", the respective services that are provided face-to-face. The increased use of telehealth and "e-services" thus has the potential to inject commercial priorities, foreign influence and trade treaty provisions directly into the health care system. By further reducing the scope of existing NAFTA and GATS protections for health care measures, such services could also expand the range of health care services to which these and subsequent trade treaty rules apply. Under existing trade treaties, a rapid expansion in the use of electronic services provided by foreign commercial providers could further restrict governments' ability to regulate in the public interest and could increase the prospects of foreign for-profit service providers in the Canadian health care system.

4.3 Unsafe practices: current health policies that increase trade treaty risks

The trade treaty problems linked to the Mazankowski and Kirby recommendations are far from academic. Since the reports were published, health care commercialization has steadily increased throughout Canada—often with foreign involvement—eroding the expression of public values Medicare represents, and incrementally allowing trade treaty rules to narrow governments' options for future health care reform.

4.3.1 Provincial approaches

The Romanow report specifically warns against a growing reliance on private delivery of diagnostic services, preferential treatment received by workers' compensation clients, and the contracting out of cataract and other surgical services. Regrettably, these practices continue throughout the country and foreign companies such as Sodexho, Compass, Aramark and Carillion are increasingly involved in delivering contracted services (see Section 4.3.4 below). Also, while the Romanow and Kirby report call for the public insurance system to be expanded, the Government of Alberta is explicitly pursuing the Mazankowski scheme of de-listing services, a regressive example that British Columbia is imitating. Alberta Premier Ralph Klein has specifically stated that his government is prepared to violate the *Canada Health Act* and that it is preparing for a "firestorm."[91] Late in 2003, the B.C. government introduced legislation to ban extra billing at private clinics and comply with the *Canada Health Act*. After passing the bill, Premier Gordon Campbell failed to give it legal effect by proclaiming it. This followed an outcry from owners of private health care clinics[92] and the installment of Prime Minister Paul Martin.[93] Both Alberta and B.C. are further corroding Medicare's sustainability by supporting for-profit delivery of publicly-insured services. The British Columbia government adopted extreme legislation to override existing public service contracts, deliberately facilitating the privatization of formerly publicly-delivered services. More recently, it legislated health care workers back to work, while imposing a 15% cut in wages and benefits of public sector health care workers and explicitly allowing for the privatization of a further 600 public sector health care jobs—a move that will further reverse pay equity gains for women that had been made in the last 30 years and establish a precedent for other provinces.[94] In Qubec, despite widespread, spirited opposition, the recently-elected government under Premier Jean Charest is proceeding with controversial changes to the province's Labour Code to permit companies and government agencies to contract out work previously performed by unionized public sector workers, and to reduce the number of bargaining units in the health system.

4.3.2 Evidence of a new federal approach to health care: P3s are 'in'

Growing support for health care privatization and commercialization is not limited to certain provincial governments. It is also becoming evident within the new federal Liberal government under Prime Minister Paul Martin.

The most recent high-profile indication that the federal approach is changing resulted from controversial comments made by Health Minister Pierre Pettigrew in late April 2004. In response to assertive questioning by New Democrat MP

Bev Desjarlais, the minister correctly told the Commons health committee that the *Canada Health Act* does not prevent for-profit companies from delivering publicly-funded health services. However, in a notable lack of balance, Mr. Pettigrew failed to mention any of the concerns about for-profit delivery including, for example, those raised in the Romanow report. Many observers judged the minister's comments and tone to signal of the government's new support for greater private for-profit health care delivery. Indeed, elaborating on his initial remarks, Minister Pettigrew appeared to echo the Mazankowski and Kirby reports:

> "If some provinces want to experiment with private delivery options, my view is that as long as [provinces] respect the single, public payer, we should be examining these efforts and then compare notes between the provinces."[95]

> "It's up to the provinces to explore in their ways of delivering [healthcare] but I'm saying that the public administration does not say everything has to be state-owned."[96]

Minister Pettigrew also indicated that he agrees with the position of certain provinces that the federal government has too much power to interpret and enforce the *Canada Health Act*:

> "My view is that the existing enforcement mechanisms just don't work… Leaving the enforcement exclusively in the hands of the federal cabinet does not really guarantee us the best possible enforcement."[97]

Pettigrew has also said he doesn't have a position on whether private MRI clinics violate the principles of medicare, potentially opening the door to more private companies keeping a share of profits when delivering publicly-funded services.[98] The current health minister's approach sharply contrasts with that of former Liberal health minister

Allan Rock, who spearheaded a federal campaign against Alberta's Bill 11, which allowed regional health authorities to contract out health care services.

The federal government has the ability to withhold federal transfers to any province that violates the *Canada Health Act*. While the federal auditor general has criticized the federal government for not living up to its obligations,[99] and public health advocates have mounted a legal challenge against Ottawa for failing to monitor provincial delivery of health services,[100] Minister Pettigrew's comments strongly suggest that the health minister will no longer use federal fiscal muscle to enforce the *Canada Health Act*. The Canadian Health Coalition's Mike McBane calls the minister's comments "extremely disturbing," adding:

> "It's a total abdication of federal authority. You can't have a national system without a minister who believes in his authority and duty to enforce national criteria."[101]

Following the media furor over his government's apparent shift in policy, Minister Pettigrew read reporters a statement asserting that his government does not favour increased private delivery within the public health system.

> "[T]he ambition of the federal government is not to encourage private delivery even within the terms of the *Canada Health Act*. Quite the contrary. Our ambition is to expand public delivery because as Roy Romanow said very well, public delivery provides Canadians with the best system possible."[102]
>
> "This government is not advocating and it is not promoting private for-profit health care."[103]

Minister Pettigrew's quick retreat has not calmed fears about the new Paul Martin Liberal government's support for greater involvement by for-profit companies in the Canadian health care system. Critics point to number of other indicators that are consistent with such support:

No blueprint for stable health-care funding

The government's February 2004 throne speech expressed concern about unacceptably long waiting lists for health care, but contained no commitments to long term and stable funding for the health care system.

The federal government's budget, released March 23, 2004 confirmed a one-time injection of $2 billion in health care funding, a commitment that had already been made to the provinces in early 2003. In response to criticism about the level of health care funding, Prime Minister Martin and Finance Minister Goodale have indicated that more long-term funding may be available when Ottawa meets with the provinces this summer. They have also indicated, without elaborating, that provinces must be willing to fundamentally change the way they deliver services.[104] In the absence of such increased funding, the pressure within provinces to privatize health care services will inevitably build. Under such circumstances, an offer of additional federal funding that is tied to P3 arrangements would be attractive to those provinces already pursuing privatization. For provinces opposed to further privatization but starved of federal funds, such an offer could prove difficult to resist.

Active P3 office in federal government

The government maintains an office within Industry Canada to provide assistance for P3s. The Public-Private Partnership (P3) Office serves as a "centre of knowledge and expertise on P3 issues." Its website asserts that "P3s offer promising new business opportunities for Canadian services firms."[105]

New Cabinet position on P3s; appointee is ardent P3 proponent

Prime Minister Martin created a new post in appointing Scarborough MP John McKay a parliamentary secretary responsible for P3s. The parliamentary secretary has indicated that there government is very active in P3 activity. For his part, as his recent public statements attest, McKay has become an enthusiastic, at times almost breathless, proponent of P3s:

> "The more I get into it, the more I realize that this is the buzz item, the big ticket. This is the way government is going to be done. I'm astounded at the amount of P3 activity which is actually going on, which I frankly wasn't aware of, and I'm impressed by the creativity that's going on between public and private partners."[106]

While no final plan on privatized services has been laid out, there is

> "a lot of noodling going on at pretty significant levels in the civil service and among public policy wonks who have all kind of unanimously come to the conclusion that we can't carry on the way we're carrying on."[107]

> "Privatization has got kind of a negative connotation. People need to be a little more nuanced and thoughtful about what privatization actually means. It will likely mean that some facilities will be privately owned and publicly available."[108]

According to the Ottawa Citizen's Bill Curry:

> "Mr. McKay said the new approach [in the Paul Martin government] will mean that every time the federal government is asked to fund something … the proposal will go through a 'P3 analysis' to see if there is a role for the private sector …"

> "'Some (projects) will clearly not be appropriate, but I expect that we will push some of the edges of creativity…. The sewer, water, all of that stuff can all be

> P3ed. Why does the government have to run a sewage system.'"
>
> "Large pension funds and merchant banks are … potential private partners for infrastructure projects. 'They are ready, willing and able to do business. All that needs to be done is a rethinking of the culture of government.'"[109 110]

Key Martin bureaucrats are P3 proponents

Prime Minister Paul Martin has appointed several P3 proponents to prominent positions in the new administration. Among them are a team of senior bureaucrats whom Mr. McKay has identified as leading the push for P3s inside the public service. These include:

- Jean-Claude Villiard, deputy minister of Industry Villiard reportedly spent three years at the World Bank in the 1990s, as the bank's Council on Infrastructure and Private Sector Development. Previously he was president of SNC-Lavalin Capital Inc., with a background in project financing.
- David Marshall, deputy minister of Public Works. Marshall was vice-chairman at CIBC before rejoining the public service in 2002.
- Kevin Lynch, deputy minister of Finance.
- McKay also reports that Treasury Board President Reg Alcock and minister of state for Infrastructure Andy Scott are strong political advocates of P3s.[111]

In April, the prime minister appointed Alberta economist Paul Boothe as an associate deputy minister of finance.[112] Mr. Boothe was a "technical advisor" to the Mazankowski Commission and a member of the Alberta Health Reform implementation team. He also led the Research Group supporting Alberta's Expert Advisory Panel to Review Publicly Funded Health Services.[113] In a December 2003 publication which he co-authored, Boothe concludes that

> "Probably the most important thing for a future prime minister could do to encourage a sustainable health system is to resist any further provincial demands for federal transfers for health care."[114]

In late January, Prime Minister Paul Martin appointed Bruce Young—a provincial and federal lobbyist who has worked on behalf of private, for-profit medical facilities—as the official responsible for British Columbia concerns in the prime minister's office. Young is a former lobbyist at the public-relations firm Hill & Knowlton, where he worked for the Coalition for Healthcare Options, a group of private, for-profit surgical and diagnostic clinics that includes one that actively promotes privatized health care. While at Hill & Knowlton, Young also worked on behalf of MDS Metro Laboratory Services, a private, for-profit laboratory testing firm.[115]

Taken together, these pieces of evidence indicate that the new federal Liberal government under Prime Minister Paul Martin displays an unprecedented level of support for public-private partnerships within Canada's health care system.

4.3.3 Examples of privatization at the provincial level

Encouraging reliance on private partners in the health sector will open the door to foreign involvement. The more governments encourage the encroachment of foreign, for-profit companies into the Canadian health care system, the more they increase the risk to citizens of expensive trade treaty litigation to reverse that trend in the future.

Unfortunately, the very danger that this analysis has identified in the three health care reports is now being steadily exacerbated, regularly and concretely, by government actions. Media reports, and government and company announcements, recently compiled by the Canadian Union of Public Employees[116], indicate that a number of provincial governments are permitting or encouraging health care privatization in a variety of ways with no effective objection from the federal government.[117] The following examples, which are drawn from the CUPE compilation, illustrate the range of privatization and commercialization initiatives that are currently underway.

For-profit hospitals and clinics

Public-private partnerships have become some provincial governments' vehicle of choice for health care commercialization. The following recent examples are illustrative of this trend.

British Columbia: Planned P3 hospital and cancer clinic

In September 2003, the British Columbia Liberal government announced a Request for Proposal for a public-private partnership for construction and operation of a private hospital and cancer centre in Abbotsford, near Vancouver. The RFP promised the winning consortium exemption from basic labour laws for more than 30 years. Four international consortia were short-listed for the project, but three dropped out. Access Health Abbotsford[118] is left as the lone bidder for the P3 project.[119] In February 2004, the Hospital Employees' Union released a summary of a review of the project RFP prepared by respected auditor Ron Parks. This report calls into question the value for money and the high potential risk burden for the public.[120]

Alberta: P3 hospitals planned for Calgary and Edmonton

In early 2003, the Calgary Health Region announced that it has issued Request for Proposals for a new private hospital in Calgary, and the Edmonton Health Authority announced plans for three P3 hospitals in that city.

Québec: considering P3 hospitals

The new Liberal government in Québec announced in June 2003 that it is considering P3 arrangements for two new "super-hospitals" in Montréal. In April 2004, a commission headed by former prime minister Brian Mulroney and former Quebec premier Daniel Johnson recommended these hospitals be P3s, and that non-clinical services also be provided through public-private partnership arrangements.[121]

New Brunswick: considering P3 hospitals

N.B. Premier Lord has stated that he favours privately owned and operated hospitals and is considering P3 arrangements for new hospitals.

Ontario: new government proceeding with P3 hospitals after all

The previous Conservative government proposed in late 2001 and 2002 to establish two P3 hospitals, in Brampton and Ottawa, which would be privately financed and operated and which would provide for-profit health care companies long-term contracts for "non-clinical" services. After sharply criticizing the P3 arrangements during the provincial election campaign, the newly-elected Liberal government is allowing the projects to proceed with only superficial changes. As planned by the previous government, a private consortium will finance and build the two hospitals and contract out maintenance, housekeeping, food and parking services, leaving public authorities to delivery core medical services. The public will make payments to the consortium to cover its costs and profits for 20-28 years. The most significant change made by the new government is minor; the facilities will be publicly-owned at the outset rather than at the conclusion of the arrangement. In effect, the public will be making mortgage payments to the consortium instead of lease payments as was originally planned. In both cases, however, the cost to the public is expected to be significantly higher than had the government financed the projects itself. [122] In March 2004, the Ontario Health Coalition and the Ontario Council of Hospital Unions released documents they say reveal that Brampton's planned hospital "is definitely a privatized P3 hospital and that all financial records, involving over $1 billion in public money, are being withheld by the hospital and the government."[123] In January, public health care advocates accused the Ontario government of secretly planning at least six more privately funded medical facilities in the province.[124] The health minister initially appeared to confirm[125] but later, in April, deny[126] this charge.

For-profit surgery, diagnostic and other specialized services

British Columbia: for-profit surgery

According to media reports published in June 2003, the Vancouver Coastal Health Authority plans to contract with for-profit companies for thousands of surgeries to be performed in private clinics. The Authority is inviting Expressions of Interest for the private delivery of up to 200 surgical services, including mastectomies, tonsillectomies, pacemaker insertions and toe amputations. The initial plan is to cover Richmond, using private clinics or private suppliers leasing space in public hospitals, and then to extend the approach throughout the region and, eventually, to other areas in B.C.

British Columbia: for-profit ambulatory care

The Vancouver General Hospital Ambulatory Care Centre will be the province's first public-private partnership arrangement (P3) involving a large health care facility. The project will be built on the Vancouver General Hospital site and will coordinate outpatient care and services. A request for proposals was issued in the summer of 2003. The winning private sector bidder will finance, design, construct and operate the facility.[127]

British Columbia: for-profit kidney dialysis and disease treatment

Baxter International, the U.S.-based multinational firm, is expected to be the company chosen by the Fraser Valley Health Region to receive the contract to manage renal care (treatment of kidney disease and dialysis) for the region. Baxter International is undergoing investigation by the U.S. Justice Department for over 50 deaths of kidney patients in five countries who used the company's dialysis services.[128]

British Columbia: for-profit cancer and heart scans

Media reports indicate that more than 1100 patients have paid $2,5000 to receive Positive Emission Tomography (PET) scans from for-profit facilities in Vancouver.[129]

Alberta: for-profit major surgery

Health Resource Centre, a for-profit surgical clinic located in Calgary, was granted approval in 2002 for providing private health services, including overnight stays, to third-party payers.[130]

Alberta: for-profit diagnostic and treatment centre

In January 2004, the Calgary Health Region announced the construction of the South Link Health Centre, which will offer "urgent care services, x-ray and laboratory services, renal dialysis, speech language therapy and a multitude of other services." Another similar centre is planned for the northwest of the city.[131]

Alberta: for-profit endoscopy procedures, knee and hip replacements, other surgical procedures

The Calgary Health Region has issued a request for expressions of interest to set up private, for-profit community outpatient clinics to provide cancer-detecting endoscopy services, which includes 8500 outpatient procedures, as well as knee and hip replacements. The region already contracts out with private, for-profit clinics for ophthalmology, oral surgery, abortions, podiatry and other surgical services. The CHR is also considering setting up private surgical facilities for foreigners and recently contracted out its payroll administration to Telus Corporation.[132]

Ontario: for-profit MRI, CT and PET clinics

Ontario sought and received bids from 43 corporations to operate 20 for-profit MRI clinics and 5 CT scan clinics. The province has reportedly opened seven for-profit MRI clinics by mid-2003, and granted rights to open 4 for-profit CAT scan clinics. According to media reports, the clinics are open for publicly-insured services only 35-40 hours per week, raising concerns that they may not shorten waiting lists. At other times, the clinics serve Worker's Compensation Board claims and patients with private health insurance. Concerns have also been raised about for-profit clinics offering as much as $10,000 bonuses to attract qualified radiologists from hospitals and public, not-for-profit providers, forcing those providers to recruit replacement staff.

In a North York medical practice, some patients reportedly pay a $2,500 membership fee for "personalized health planning" that includes shorter waits for MRI scans.

A for-profit Positron Emission Tomography (PET) clinic was opened in Mississauga in March, 2003.

Ontario: P3 considered for addiction treatment

The province and the board of the Centre for Addiction and Mental Health is reportedly considering a P3 arrangement as part of the amalgamation of four Toronto treatment sites. Staff have reportedly been advised to shift reporters' and other questioners' attention away the P3 issue.[133]

Nova Scotia: for-profit MRI clinics

Three new for-profit MRI clinics were operating in early 2003, with a fourth scheduled to open late in the year.

For-profit administration, food, cleaning and other health-related services

British Columbia: For-profit administration of public health insurance system

The British Columbia government announced in July 2003 that it was seeking bids from private companies to take over the day-to-day running of the B.C. Medical Services Plan, the provincial public insurance system, and its Pharmacare program. On March 31, 2004, the B.C. government announced that it had selected U.S.-based Maximus, Inc. for this purpose and would enter into negotiations with the company to conclude a final contract in August.[134]

The B.C. Government and Service Employees' Union (BCGEU) filed an application for a judicial review of the decision on February 24, 2004. The union contends that the arrangement violates the "public administration" pillar of the *Canada Health Act*. It has also filed expert opinion stating that the under the so-called USA Patriot Act, the FBI could gain access to British Columbians' MSP records, including information on health treatment, pharmacy, income tax, mental health and criminal records, and records from the ministries of children and family development and human resources. The opinion states that U.S. legal precedents suggest that even if the information is held by a Canadian subsidiary, its U.S. parent company could be required to disclose the information to the FBI, and could be prohibited from revealing that it had done so.[135]

British Columbia: for-profit food, cleaning, laundry, and housekeeping services

The Vancouver Coastal Health Authority laid off 850 unionized workers in Vancouver hospitals after signing a 5-year contract with a for-profit corporation to supply cleaning and infection control services in operating rooms, intensive care units and other specialized hospital settings. The VCHA is reportedly also pursuing contracts with for-profit companies for food services.

The Vancouver Island Health Authority is reportedly pursuing contracts with for-profit companies for housekeeping and food services in hospitals and other health care facilities in the region.

The Fraser Health Authority has contracted with a for-profit company to provide centralized laundry services; laundry from near Vancouver is currently being trucked to and from Alberta.

Alberta: for-profit ambulance services

Edmonton's Capital Health contracted with a for-profit company to provide ambulance services.

Quebec: new legislation facilitates for-profit health services

The recently-elected Quebec government invoked closure to limit debate and used an all-night legislative session to pass a controversial series of laws in a stormy legislative sitting that ended in mid-December, 2003. The bills passed included Bill 31, which amends the section of Quebec's Labour Code that now limits the contracting-out of work covered by union collective agreements.[136] Under the changes, which come into force on February 1, 2004, companies or government agencies will be permitted to contract out work previously performed by public sector workers to for-profit subcontractors who are not required to adhere to the salary and working conditions specified in the original union collective agreement.[137]

Ontario considering more P3s in "ancillary" health services

In April 2004, Ontario Health Minister George Smitherman signaled his government's intent to press on with further P3s. He noted that the changes the government made to the Brampton and Ottawa P3 arrangements (see above) "does not mean that there isn't room for the private sector to play a role in the delivery of ancillary services." The Toronto Star reported that Public Infrastructure Renewal Minister David Caplan is "wide open to private funding of public hospitals."[138]

Ontario: new bill would grant Minister sweeping powers to restructure health service delivery

Ontario's new health minister introduced Bill 8, the Commitment to the Future of Medicare Act, on November 27, 2003.[139] This bill, which has received second reading,[140] would make it illegal for people to pay to receive faster access to publicly-insured health services, and for health care practitioners to accept extra payment for these services. This aspect of the bill provides a commendable example for other provinces. In addition, however, the accountability provisions in Part III of the bill would grant the Minister the authority to compel health care service providers to enter into compliance agreements—to reduce the budgets of hospitals, long term care facilities and community care agencies, for example.[141] Depending on how these sweeping powers are administered, they could have two important effects. They could allow the government to cancel existing or pending P3 contracts without facing domestic legal action by affected corporations.[142] They could also allow the government, with legal impunity, to issue compliance orders that would force fundamental restructuring of hospital service delivery, including the "rationalization" of services, with little public scrutiny.

For-profit home care, retirement home and assisted living services

Saskatchewan: for-profit care homes

The elimination of restrictions on the number of beds in homes, together with a decline in the number of publicly-funded beds, reportedly has lead to an expansion in certain types of for profit personal care homes. Approximately 60 publicly-funded beds have been closed in the last few years, and the number of privately-funded beds, together with a range of accompanying services, has increased across the province.[143]

Ontario: for-profit home care services

Ontario's competitive bidding model has resulted in increases of for-profit home care service delivery at the expense of not-for-profit providers across the province. Private companies are guaranteed a steady income of public dollars in contracts that may be of 20 years duration. Mandatory resident fees have increased and a prominent media report refers to "a government-sanctioned shift toward 'preferred' residents able to pay semi-private and private room fees."[144]

The above list indicates that a broad array of services that span the health care system are, or could soon be, commercialized or privatized. These services range from food, cleaning, laundry and housecleaning services to homecare services; from diagnostic scans to records management; and from surgery to the management of hospitals and the administration of public health insurance. Prominent companies involved in supplying or bidding for these services include the following:[145]

- Carillion Canada Inc. Its parent company, U.K.-based Carillion Plc, specializes in the supply of newly-privatized services.[146]
- Compass Group Canada. Its parent company, U.K.-based Compass Group Plc is one of the world's largest food and contracted service companies. Compass subsidiaries are active in Ontario, Newfoundland, Nova Scotia and B.C.[147]
- Sodexho Canada. Its parent company Sodexho Inc. is one of the three largest "outsourcing" service corporations in North America, supplying food, housekeeping and laundry services.[148]
- Aramark Canada Ltd. U.S.-based Aramark has operations in 18 countreis, supplying prison, food, housekeeping and daycare services. It also offers a range of other services, including media management, human resources, records management, and information technology.[149]

The increasing involvement of these companies, and the creeping commercialization it represents, is occurring despite the clear warnings in the Romanow report that it threatens key aspects of Medicare.

Foreign service corporations operating along the margins and in the very heart of the Canadian health care system can use trade treaty rules to consolidate their commercial position. Under the shadow of international trade treaties, the health care commercialization illustrated in the afore-mentioned examples can no longer be characterized as easily-reversible policy experiments. Increasing commercialization now threatens to ensnare Canadian health policy in a complex web of binding international rules designed specifically to facilitate international business. Regrettably, most local health authorities and governments at all levels that are engaged in this commercialization – and Canadian citizens generally – have little, if any, appreciation of the power of these trade treaty rules to 'lock-in' health care commercialization.

4.4 Looming challenges of even more expansive trade treaties

The more intrusive and potent trade treaties become, the more hazardous they can be to Medicare and other public services systems. The most significant new risks are now posed by ongoing, previously-mandated negotiations on the GATS, and by negotiations to conclude a proposed Free Trade Areas of the Americas (FTAA).

4.4.1 GATS negotiations

The GATS contains a feature that is especially relevant to future health care reform. It has built into its structure an overarching commitment for repeated re-negotiations to increase the treaty's coverage. Canada and other GATS members have already agreed to this open-ended, ratchet-like commitment to ever-higher levels of liberalization. While few members have so far specifically agreed to list health measures, over the long term, pressure to apply GATS rules more extensively in the health sector poses a grave threat to health care development and reform both in Canada and elsewhere.

Ongoing GATS negotiations to expand the treaty threaten health care reform in several general ways[150].

Legal uncertainty and misunderstanding about key aspects of the treaty

Firstly, basic misunderstandings about the complex treaty increase the risk that some governments may inadvertently apply GATS rules to health care services. For example, WTO officials and developed country negotiators have made reassuring but misleading statements that could encourage unwary governments to believe, wrongly, that public services are fully excluded from the treaty. This uncertainty could cause governments to make new or more expansive specific commitments that unintentionally expose important aspects of the health care system to successful GATS challenge.

Secondly, secretive treaty negotiations can provide governments political cover for making unpopular regulatory changes in the sensitive health care sector. They can also facilitate governments' efforts in "overcoming domestic resistance to change"[151]

Thirdly, the treaty contains important provisions that are unclear and about which members disagree and which will ultimately be clarified by unelected WTO dispute panelists. The treaty grants these individuals the ability to rule on such key issues even though most panelists have little expertise in health care policy and have no legitimate authority for balancing often-competing public policy priorities.

Constant pressure for new, more extensive GATS commitments

In the current and future rounds of GATS re-negotiations, governments will face intense pressure to make new, more extensive specific commitments. In the longer term, this pressure will almost certainly extend to health-related services. For example, firms seeking expanded markets overseas often apply pressure on their governments to use the GATS negotiations to obtain market-opening concessions in other countries. Also, foreign firms apply similar pressure on their governments to extract equivalent concessions in Canada. Such pressure can be strong and hard to resist.

Canadian representatives have repeatedly stated that Canada will make no GATS commitments covering health care in this round of negotiations. However, as one of the strongest proponents of GATS expansion, Canada is likely to come under increasing pressure, both in the current round and in future rounds of re-negotiations, to make GATS requests and offers affecting services that are integral to the Canadian health care system. This pressure will become even more pronounced as, in future rounds, health becomes one of the few remaining sectors where Canada has not taken commitments. As unfavourable trade rulings involving Canadian cultural policy have shown, such constant pressure can be difficult to resist successfully over long periods of time, even in areas that, like health, are particularly politically sensitive and important to the public.

Moreover, once any single future Canadian federal government yields to this pressure, the GATS makes it very difficult for subsequent governments to reverse course. In this way, the treaty interferes unacceptably with the normal ebb and flow of decision-making in a democratic system of government.[152]

Pressure for other GATS concessions: proposed restrictions on domestic regulation.

GATS re-negotiations that are now underway entail other threats to Canada's health care system. The most important of these is the proposed "disciplines" on governments' domestic regulation. These proposed rules have a number of features that could give them extraordinary power.[153]

The proposed rules would comprise a new, distinct class of GATS rules. They would be intended to act like a fine-meshed drift net — capturing government measures not caught by other GATS constraints. For example, even government measures that are consistent both with the tough non-discrimination rules contained in the GATS and the treaty's market access provisions could still be found to violate the new domestic regulation restrictions.

The proposed new rules would also cover subject matter that is very broad and highly relevant to health care services. They would extend to "measures relating to qualification requirements and procedures, technical standards and licensing procedures"[154]. While these terms are not defined precisely in the treaty, they can be expected to include, for example, the accreditation of doctors and other professionals, and the licensing and certification of hospitals and clinics. The provision's reach could be lengthened further by a broad interpretation of the term "technical standards." According to the WTO Secretariat, the term refers not just to the "technical characteristics of the service itself" but also to "the rules according to which the service must be performed."[155]

Significantly, the proposed restrictions are intended to apply a test of "necessity" to measures covered by this broad provision. That is, governments would face the difficult onus of demonstrating that their regulations affecting the health care system were "necessary" to achieve a legitimate objective. Governments would also have to prove that no alternative measure was available that was less commercially restrictive. While the precise application of these concepts is now under negotiation, there can be little doubt that the intent is for their application to capture a very wide range of government regulations.[156]

Also, though it is a matter for negotiation, it is possible that the proposed GATS domestic regulation rules will apply across-the-board to all measures, even to those for which members have made no specific commitments.[157]

Finally, whatever domestic regulation rules are agreed to during negotiations, they are likely to apply without exception, since the article does not allow for any country-specific exceptions or limitations.[158] While the rules will not themselves establish global standards, they would ensure that domestic health care standards and practices meet GATS rules – without exception.

Together, these features indicate that the GATS domestic regulation negotiations could soon bring public health care systems even further within the purview of the WTO. If the negotiations proceed as expected, the resulting rules would allow dispute panels to oversee an extraordinarily broad range of domestic procedures and standards to ensure they meet GATS rules. These panels could second-guess policies concerning many important aspects of Medicare. The GATS negotiations on domestic regulation, that are now well underway, thus pose a serious threat to the regulatory underpinnings of Canada's public health care system.

4.4.2 FTAA and other negotiations

At the recent FTAA ministerial meeting held in Miami in late November, ministers of the 34 countries negotiating a hemispheric free trade agreement scaled back their plans for the final stage of negotiations. At the insistence of Brazil, the other Mercosur countries and Venezuela, ministers agreed to work towards a so-called "two-tier" agreement. According to the

Ministerial Declaration,[159] the FTAA negotiating committee will:

> "develop a common and balanced set of rights and obligations applicable to all countries" that will include provisions in each of the following areas: "market access; agriculture; services; investment; government procurement; intellectual property; competition policy; subsidies, antidumping, and countervailing duties; and dispute settlement."

In addition,

> "[o]n a plurilateral basis, interested parties may choose to develop additional liberalization and disciplines."

Consequently, the main focus on negotiations in the immediate future will be defining "what core obligations will constitute the 'balance of rights and obligations' and what 'additional obligations and benefits' will be optional."[160]

The Canadian government, however, continues to very strongly support a comprehensive FTAA with NAFTA-type, or "NAFTA-plus," obligations covering all sectors including services, investment intellectual property, and government procurement. Obligations in these sectors pose the greatest risks to Canada's health care system. Even if the FTAA ultimately contains certain optional obligations in these key areas, it is very likely that the Canadian government will agree to be bound by them.

In fact, Canada has already made an offer to cover services and investment in the FTAA and this offer remains on the table. This initial offer, together with drafts of the services and investment chapters,[161] indicate that the Canadian government is pursuing an FTAA that combines the most intrusive features of the NAFTA investment chapter and the GATS services provisions.

The Canadian government continues to support incorporating many of the most controversial features of the NAFTA investment chapter into the FTAA, including:

- investor-state dispute settlement,
- broad expropriation-compensation provisions,
- minimum standard of treatment rules, and
- performance requirements prohibitions.

Moreover, the draft FTAA services chapter also includes some significant "NAFTA-plus" provisions drawn from the GATS. For example:

- The FTAA services chapter (Article 7, Market access) would prohibit monopolies in all covered sectors, and
- the FTAA services chapter (Article 5) would apply national treatment to subsidies (by contrast, subsidies are exempted from NAFTA's national treatment rule).

The impacts of these NAFTA-plus features drawn from the GATS would be compounded by the approach, again strongly supported by Canada, that the FTAA services chapter be "top-down."

Combining these tough NAFTA-plus provisions with a top-down approach obviously dictates that Canadian negotiators take a fresh, serious look at the potential for challenges to the Canadian health care measures and to develop new more strongly worded reservations to protect the Canadian health care system. Yet, Canada's proposed FTAA reservation for health and social services is exactly the same as its flawed 1994 NAFTA reservation. Canada's reservation does not even, for example, provide any protection against the controversial expropriation claims, which many trade experts and the Romanow Commission agree poses a serious threat to the reform and renewal of the Canadian health care system.

4.4.3 Conclusion

Each successive set of multilateral, regional and bilateral trade and investment negotiations makes the task of protecting Canada's health care system from erosion more difficult. Each agreement sets precedents for more intrusive provisions in the next. These cascading negotiations subject Canada to continuous pressure to weaken or even remove vital exceptions and reservations for health care. Unless this harmful dynamic is changed, the further erosion of protection for health care becomes only a matter of time. The next chapter of this book explores new trade policy approaches and strategies that are needed to effectively safeguard Canadians ability to preserve and strengthen our public, not-for-profit health care system over the long term.

CHAPTER 5

Towards *healthy* health care reform

AS ANALYSTS AND ADVOCATES on all sides of the issues have repeatedly emphasised, the Canadian health care system is at a crossroads. One of the central and recurring themes in the debate over its future is whether private financing and for-profit provision of health care should play a greater role in the Canadian health care system, as it does in our giant neighbour to the south?[162]

An examination of Canada's trade and investment treaty obligations and the scope of the exemptions for health care under those treaties, adds an absolutely crucial dimension to this important debate. It reveals that Canada's trade treaty commitments threaten to make commercialising reforms difficult and costly to reverse: basically a one-way street.[163]

All of the three major reports we have analysed take strong positions on the appropriate role of private financing and for-profit delivery. Both Mazankowski and Kirby clearly regard Canadians' substantial investment in health care as a rich commercial opportunity for the private sector. Both assert that subjecting the health care sector to entrepreneurial values and market discipline is necessary to modernize it. Mazankowski envisages a significantly expanded role for both private financing and for-profit delivery, while Kirby generally adheres to the principle of public financing (even envisioning expanding the medicare monopoly to new services) while embracing market-based mechanisms and an expanded private sector role in delivery.

Romanow, by contrast, vigorously supports renewing Medicare around the core principles of public financing and not-for-profit delivery. The Romanow report advocates a significant expansion of the public insurance monopoly to cover new services, strongly rejects a for-profit role in the delivery of core health services, and asserts that the inroads already made by for-profit providers in key areas such as diagnostic services be rolled back. Yet even Romanow, in a concession to the forceful privatization lobby, leaves the door open to an expanded private sector role in the delivery of so-called ancillary health services.[164]

Both the Mazankowski and Kirby reports are conspicuously silent about the potential impact of trade treaties on the health care system and their proposed reforms. It is barely conceivable that such issues never came to their attention. The impact of trade treaties became a public issue during the controversial debate over Alberta's privatization legislation.[165] There has been a lively and extended debate about the scope of the NAFTA exemptions and the impact of the GATS in the legal and scholarly community. Moreover, the Romanow Commission reported that the impact of trade treaties on medicare was raised at almost every public meeting convened by the commission.[166] The issue is clearly in the public domain and its glaring omission from major reports can only be deliberate.

One of the main purposes of the services and investment provisions of modern trade treaties is to lock in commercializing reforms and to prevent "backsliding" by future governments that might seek to reverse failed market-based reforms. Because both Mazankowski and Kirby embrace, to varying degrees, market-based reform, they would almost certainly regard locking in these initiatives through trade treaties with approval. Suppressing the uncomfortably anti-democratic consequences of trade treaty impacts on health care reform is self-serving.

The Romanow report, by contrast, explicitly engages the issue of trade treaties potential impact on health care reform. Because of the report's strong commitment to the public, not-for-profit character of medicare it is not surprising that it regards trade treaties as a legitimate cause for concern. The Romanow report alone begins with the responsible and incontestable argument, that "any decisions about expanding private for-profit delivery could have implications under international trade agreements that need to be considered in advance."[167]

Our study has analysed in depth the potential impacts of trade treaties on the health care reform recommendations contained in all three major reports. Despite the significant threats that these treaty provisions pose, it is our view that Canadian health care reform can navigate these risks. But to do so successfully will require new initiatives on a range of policy fronts. It will require: careful planning of future health care reforms to avoid trade treaty problems; fundamental changes in Canadian trade policy strategies and negotiating objectives; and new thinking and creative diplomacy to achieve a better balance in the international system between promoting health as a public good and protecting commercial and trading interests.

5.1 Minimizing trade risks while avoiding 'regulatory chill' in health care reform

Careful, advance consideration of trade treaty risks is a vital component of health care reform. It should always been borne in mind that it is primarily the public, not-for profit character of Canada's health care system – not the flawed trade treaty exemptions for health – that insulate it from trade challenges. If this defining character is eroded, the risk of trade litigation will grow in inverse proportion. Ill-considered health care reform initiatives that lead to greater commercialization and foreign involvement in Canada's health care system will greatly increase Canadians' exposure to future trade treaty challenges.

5.1.1 Expanding Medicare coverage

From a trade treaty perspective, the sooner the widely supported proposals to expand public insurance to embrace new services such as homecare or prescription drugs occur, the better. The possibility of a NAFTA investor-state challenge alleging that expanding public insurance "expropriates" private insurers' investments is real, although its outcome cannot be predicted with certainty. Also, Canada's GATS commitments covering private health insurance provide foreign insurers with recourse through their home governments to GATS dispute settlement.

But the risk of these trade challenges also needs to be kept in perspective. Canada's exposure to foreign investors' and service providers treaty claims is, in most instances, not yet that extreme. This is because, while health care commercialization in Canada is clearly proliferating, its scale of is still limited, and the level of foreign involvement is smaller still.[168] Only foreign interests have enforceable rights under trade treaties.

As the Romanow report observes,

> "Rather than conclude ... that Canada is hemmed in to the current system and cannot change, the more reasonable conclusion is that if we want to expand the range of services in the public system, it is better to do it now while there still is very little foreign presence in health care in Canada and the potential costs of [trade] compensation are low."[169]

While real, the risks of trade treaty litigation should not be used as a pretext to thwart essential health care reform. Canada has a window of opportunity to expand its public health insurance system, but unless action is taken soon that window could close.

5.1.2 Public, not-for-profit delivery

Because of its vast and decentralised character, the delivery side of health care services is far more susceptible to creeping commercialization. Inevitably, initiatives to increase private, for-profit delivery will attract foreign commercial involvement — increasing the risk of future trade treaty litigation. Canada is situated next to the largest private, for-profit health care industry in the world. For both political and economic motives, the US industry is eager to expand into the Canadian health care system.

In *Putting Health First*, the CCPA research consortium described this dangerous interaction of commercializing reforms and trade treaty obligations as a "vicious circle."

> "The trend towards increasing commercialization in health care—through private financing, market-based models for allocating funding, and for-profit delivery of services—raises particularly troubling trade policy issues. Such commercialization threatens to set in motion a self-reinforcing dynamic—a vicious circle—that could undermine the foundations of Canada's Medicare system. Commercialization weakens

> the protective effect of trade treaty safeguards for health at the same time that it facilitates the entry of foreign investors and service providers into newly created markets in health services. The greater the presence of foreign investors and services providers, the greater the possibility of trade disputes if governments take actions that limit or reverse foreign penetration. Thus, once foreign investors and service providers become involved in Canada's health care system—and the more involved they become—the more difficult and costly it will be to limit or reverse the trend towards commercialization in general."[170]

Unfortunately, this "vicious circle" may already be in play in Ontario. The newly-elected provincial government reneged on its pledge cancel P3 hospital contracts negotiated in the dying days of the previous Conservative regime. While the facts may never be publicly known, the potential for NAFTA investor-state litigation may have played a role in the government's decision to implement only superficial changes to those arrangements. If the government had cancelled the contracts, and if, as reported, the contracts included participation by U.S. interests, threatened NAFTA investor-state litigation would have been virtually certain, and actual cases may have followed. Given its repeated, emphatic assurances that health care is beyond the reach of NAFTA, the federal government is obliged to defend vigorously against any such NAFTA claim in the future and bear full responsibility for any compensation if it subsequently loses.

Steps should be taken now to avoid such unsavoury challenges to democratically decided health care reform in future. As a crucial first step, governments at all levels should not proceed with so-called public-private partnerships in health care and should avoid P3 arrangements in the future. Instead, governments should take measures to strengthen the public, not-for-profit character of the Canadian health care system which, if taken promptly, would insulate Canadians from future trade treaty challenges. The "vicious circle" precipitated by commercialization can be supplanted by a "virtuous circle."

Strictly avoiding commercialization maximises the protection afforded by the existing trade treaty exemptions. It also curbs the stake of all for-profit providers and investors in the Canadian health care system, and thereby minimizes the stake of foreign for-profit providers and investors (who alone enjoy rights under commercial trade treaties). General measures to reduce commercialisation where it already exists, and to prevent it from encroaching on the pubic, not-for-profit aspects of the system, achieves protection from trade treaty litigation, without discriminating against foreign investors or service providers.

Health reforms should be fashioned to make the most benefit of existing safeguards in NAFTA and the GATS by introducing measures most closely corresponding to the standard public service model. This means minimizing the role of private financing and for-profit service delivery by:

- Extending universal access to services on the basis of need, rather than ability to pay or other criteria;
- Establishing clear public purpose objectives and regulations;
- Financing services out of public revenue;
- Favouring direct subsidies or grants over contracted services; and
- Where services are contracted, adopting standard government procurement procedures.[171]

These kinds of measures are most likely to be shielded from the various NAFTA and GATS provisions. They consequently preserve government flexibility to modify policies, whereas market-oriented reforms are more likely to trigger trade obligations that would restrict public policy flexibility.[172]

A formidable challenge in the Canadian federal system is that commercializing reforms take place at the provincial or local level, while the responsibility for enforcing the principles of the *Canada Health Act* rests with the federal government. The federal government has, so far, failed to vigorously enforce the letter or the spirit of the Act.[173] This laissez-faire approach invites trade treaty problems.

Avoiding commercialization of health services—and taking prompt action to contain or reverse existing commercialization— is good public policy. It also has the benefit of reducing the risk of future trade treaty challenges.

5.2 Relieving pressure on health: changing the approach to trade treaties

As discussed, there is an inherent tension between the public policy objectives of Medicare — that is, providing care to all on the basis of need rather than ability to pay — and the commercializing imperatives of modern trade and investment treaties. The Canadian health care system is a mixed public-private system. With regard to trade and investment treaties, the goal must be to preserve the ability of governments to closely regulate Canada's entire mixed health care system: including its public, private not-for-profit and private for-profit components. Governments' ability to shift this mix – without fear of becoming entangled in trade disputes and threat of sanctions – should be fully protected.

Canada's current exemptions in NAFTA and the GATS, while they do provide some protection, are flawed and inadequate. Concerted changes in Canada's existing trade policy commitments and its objectives in ongoing negotiations will be necessary to secure strong, fully effective protection for health care and to relieve the distorting pressure that trade treaties exert on the Canadian health care system and its future reform.

Several concurrent shifts are desirable. Those existing commitments that already pose a threat to health care reform need to be changed. In order to achieve more effective safeguards for health in ongoing and future negotiations, Canada's negotiating goals and strategies should be overhauled. Finally, Canada should champion longer-term changes in the international system to assure that health protection and promotion no longer takes a back seat to the protection and promotion of commercial rights.

5.2.1 Changes to existing treaty commitments

It is generally acknowledged that the NAFTA expropriation and compensation provisions pose the most serious trade treaty threat to Canadian health reforms.[174] Less widely understood, is that Canada's GATS commitments covering heath insurance are also a serious obstacle to the future expansion of public health insurance coverage.

Both these problems need to be remedied:

- Canada should negotiate a binding interpretation of NAFTA's investment chapter to narrow the meaning of expropriation to be consistent with that under Canadian law.
- If Canada fails to get agreement to do so from other NAFTA parties, it should strongly assert its own view that expanding public health insurance is not a compensable expropriation under domestic or international law and that NAFTA's investment rules will not be permitted to interfere with Canadian health care reforms.
- Canada should abandon its support of the NAFTA investor-state dispute settlement mechanism and instead seek its elimination in NAFTA and in bilateral investment treaties.

- Canada should withdraw its existing GATS commitment covering health insurance. The GATS Article XXI provides a means for countries to withdraw commitments upon negotiating "compensatory adjustments" in its GATS coverage. The sooner Canada invokes this process, the less difficult and costly it will be.

Withdrawing GATS commitments will be contentious, but the process is relatively straightforward. By contrast, curtailing the threat from the NAFTA investor-state mechanism and its extreme expropriation provisions is a more daunting task.

Other existing provisions of the NAFTA investment and services chapters and of the GATS, including core rules such as national treatment, market access and the prohibition of performance requirements, also pose potential problems for the regulation and reform of the Canadian health care system. To insulate against these Canada also needs to strengthen its existing NAFTA reservations, either through negotiation or by simply asserting its determination that health care reform will not be frustrated by NAFTA harassment. Likewise, Canada should support efforts to secure a fully effective GATS carve-out for public service systems, including health care, either by strengthening the ineffectual "governmental authority" exclusion or through other means.

5.2.2 Overhauling Canada's trade negotiating objectives

Despite recent setbacks in Cancun and Miami, the Canadian government remains an enthusiastic and relatively uncritical supporter of further trade and investment treaty expansion. Canada is actively engaged in negotiations to create a Free Trade Area of the Americas (FTAA), some regional free trade agreements, and in the WTO Doha Round, which includes many health-related matters including services, investment, and intellectual property. Canada should adopt a precautionary approach to prevent further exposure of our health care system to increased pressure and possible challenge.

Although the Canadian government continues to insist that health care is "off the table" and "non-negotiable" in all these arenas, the very breadth and complexity of the new trade and investment treaty agenda, combined with shortcomings in Canada's approach to exempting health policy measures, makes the validity of such assurances highly questionable.

The FTAA services and investment negotiations provide a case in point. The draft negotiating services text contains NAFTA-plus features,[175] supported by Canada, that would pose even more formidable problems for Canada's health care system. Despite this looming threat and rising concern about flaws in the NAFTA reservations, the Canadian government in its opening offer on services and investment simply recycled an exact carbon copy of the flawed NAFTA reservations for health and social services. When it comes to safeguarding health, Canadian negotiators actions speak louder than their words.

Wherever conflicts between health and commercial policy persist, Canada should not rely exclusively on country-specific social exceptions, which have significant shortcomings and should be regarded only as stopgap measures. Instead, Canada should pursue generally agreed exceptions or safeguards—permanent features of treaties that are far more likely to endure over time.

To this end:

- Canadian negotiators should be directed to pursue a self-defining exemption for health polices in all its international trade and investment agreements.
- Canada should lodge a new exception in its GATS schedule (a "horizontal limitation") making clear that no commitment in any sector affects the Canadian health care system or Canada's ability to regulate to protect the health of Canadians.

- In ongoing negotiations such as under the GATS and the proposed FTAA, Canada should not make commitments covering any aspect of the health care system (e.g. telehealth, health information systems, or hospital management) or that affect its ability to regulate for health purposes (e.g. distribution of prescription drugs, tobacco or alcohol).
- To be a good global citizen and to minimize future pressure on Canada to cover health, Canada should make no requests of other countries to cover any health-related services or that affect their ability to regulate for health purposes.[176]

In short, the federal government must change its current approach to trade treaties—whether NAFTA, FTAA or GATS –which promotes unbalanced treaties that perpetually increase commercializing pressure on Canada's health care system. The federal government should begin by acknowledging the existing threats to public service systems and public interest regulation, and changing its trade negotiating objectives and existing treaty commitments to secure the strong, fully effective protection for Medicare that Canadians were promised, but not given.

5.2.3 Rebalancing the right to health and the protection of commercial interests in the international system

Over the longer term, Canada should champion new international health protection treaties that supersede commercial trade agreements. It should also reinvigorate its commitment to enforce existing commitments to health as a human right under human rights treaties and covenants to which Canada is already a signatory.[177] The gross disparity between the powerful enforcement of trade and investment treaties and the lack of effective sanctions to enforce the right to health is evidence of the underdeveloped nature of international systems of governance. If global economic cooperation is to be sustainable, then those imbalances in the international system that give far greater priority to commercial and investor rights than to basic human rights, such as the right to health, must be corrected.

The Romanow report recommendation to build alliances within the international community to achieve such changes is an encouraging start. Canada should work in multilateral forums to forge agreements in the area of human rights, environment, and health that are enforceable and, where they conflict, supersede the rules in agreements like the WTO and NAFTA. Examples of treaties that attempt to reach these goals are the Montreal Bio-safety Protocol, the Stockholm Convention on Persistent Organic Pollutants, the Framework on Tobacco Control, and the Cultural Diversity Instrument initiative, where the Canadian government is taking the lead.

Endnotes

1 This fundamental point is highlighted in the report prepared for the Romanow Commission by a consortium on globalization and health, which was organized by the Canadian Centre for Policy Alternatives.

Putting Health First: Canadian Health Care Reform, Trade Treaties and Foreign Policy, Canadian Centre for Policy Alternatives Consortium on Globalization and Health, Summary Report, Commission on the Future of Health Care in Canada, October, 2002. Available at: http://www.hc-sc.gc.ca/english/pdf/romanow/pdfs/Summary_Globalization_E.pdf and http://www.policyalternatives.ca/publications/putting-health-first.pdf .

2 Other treaties, including the World Trade Organization treaties on Technical Barriers to Trade (TBT) and Sanitary and Phytosanitary (SPS) measures, and numerous bilateral investment treaties (BITs), may also be relevant, but are beyond the scope of this book.

3 This section draws heavily upon the summary provided in *Putting Health First*, *supra*, endnote 1.

4 Existing, non-conforming *local* government measures are also grand-parented under NAFTA Article 1108.1.iii.

[5] When NAFTA was first signed, provincial and state governments were given until January 1, 1996 to identify any existing, non-conforming measures that they wished to maintain and to list them specifically under Annex I. Because of the sweeping scope of the chapters and the inherent uncertainty about the meaning of its broadly worded rules, the process of identifying potentially non-conforming measures proved to be very difficult. After several postponements of the deadline, the three federal governments agreed to set aside the provisional lists of subnational non-conforming measures and instead to submit a single, general reservation that exempted all existing non-conforming provincial and state measures. Concerns raised by provincial and state governments, as well as unions, NGOs and public interest advocacy groups, about the potential impacts of the NAFTA investment and services chapters on health care services were a key factor in pressing the decision to proceed via a general reservation instead of a narrower list of specific non-conforming measures.

[6] For a fuller discussion of bound and unbound reservations see Appleton, Barry, 1994, *Navigating NAFTA: A Concise Users' Guide to the North American Free Trade Agreement*, Carswell, pp. 161 ff.

[7] The U.S. and Mexico took virtually identical Annex II reservations for health and social services.

[8] For a discussion of the differing views of Canadian and U.S. governments during the NAFTA sub-national reservations exercise, see *Putting Health First*, supra, endnote 1, pp. 13 15 and *Inside NAFTA*, November 29, 1995.

[9] Sanger, Matthew, 2001, *Reckless Abandon: Canada, the GATS and the Future of Health* Care, Canadian Centre for Policy Alternatives, pp. 77 ff.

10 Both NAFTA and the GATS contain general exceptions (NAFTA Article 2101 and GATS Article XIV) that allow governments to argue that otherwise inconsistent measures are necessary to achieve legitimate objectives, including protection of human health. These general exceptions have, however, been interpreted quite restrictively by trade dispute panels. NAFTA's general exception does not apply to the NAFTA investment chapter.

11 The earlier Canada-U.S. Free Trade Agreement also included some services and investment provisions, but these have been superseded by the NAFTA.

12 Cf. World Trade Organization, GATS section of "Trading into the Future: An on-line guide to the WTO Agreements," available at www.wto.org.

13 This is because the Annex II-C-9 reservation does not apply against Article 1103 (MFN), while the NAFTA Annex I general reservation for existing, non-conforming measures does.

14 See NAFTA Articles 1108.7 and 1201.2.d.

15 Sanger, Matthew; Shrybman, Steven; and Lexchin, Joel, 2002, "Implications of Canada's international trade commitments for health policy and health reform options," Research Report prepared for the Commission on the Future of Health Care in Canada, 1.1.1

16 NAFTA's monopoly rules apply only to federal monopolies (NAFTA Article 1505), while the GATS applies to both federal and provincial monopolies. The NAFTA's expropriation and compensation provisions, however, apply to provincial as well as federal measures.

17 Sanger, Shrybman, and Lexchin, 2002, *supra*, endnote 14, 1.2.9.

[18] A compulsory license allows another manufacturer, upon payment of royalties to the patent holder, to produce generic copies of a patented drug.

[19] Canadian Institute for Health Information, 2002, *Drug Expenditure in Canada, 1985-2001*, Ottawa, Canadian Institute for Health Information, cited in: The report of the Commission on the Future of Health Care, (Romanow Report), 2002, p. 196.

[20] Derfel, Aaron, "Drug costs will soar in FTAA: experts," Montreal Gazette, April 18, 2001.

[21] GATS Article XVI.

[22] NAFTA Article 1207 provides for further negotiations on these lists, but these have never occurred. Local government measures need not be listed.

[23] Luff, David, Regulation of Health Services and International Trade Law, paper prepared for the OECD-World Bank Services Experts Meeting, OECD, Paris, March 4-5, 2002., para. 128

[24] Cf. Luff, op. cit., paras. 148 ff.

[25] While the GATS does not explicitly prohibit performance requirements, its national treatment principle implicitly prevents governments from applying local content, sourcing and other performance requirements to foreign service providers in covered sectors.

[26] This Annex II reservation does apply against Article 1205, enabling Canadian governments to adopt or maintain measures to require service providers to establish in Canada as a condition for the "cross-border" provision of a service (Article 1205).

[27] Cf. Johnson, J.R., 2002, How will international trade agreements affect Canadian health care?, Discussion Paper prepared for the Commission on the Future of Health Care in Canada, p.18.

[28] Sanger, Shrybman, and Lexchin, 2002, *supra*, endnote 14, 1.1.5.

[29] Furthermore, in the Metalclad case the investor argued successfully that the minimum standards of treatment provisions entitled the investor to a standard of treatment expressed not in NAFTA chapter 11, but in a separate part of the NAFTA. Subsequently, other investors have used this opening to argue that other provisions in NAFTA, and even in the WTO agreements, can be indirectly enforced through NAFTA chapter 11. In July, 2001 the NAFTA Commission, comprised of the three trade ministers, adopted an interpretation, based on a traditional customary international law interpretation of minimum international standards. This interpretative note was intended to restrict investors to enforcing only NAFTA chapter 11 through the investor-state process. It remains to be seen how arbitral panels will implement this note.

[30] The existing WTO agreements contain no comparable investment protection provisions.

[31] In the words of the Metalclad panel, "expropriation under NAFTA includes not only open, deliberate and acknowledged takings of property … but also covert or incidental interference with the use of property which has the effect of depriving the owner, in whole or in significant part, of the use or reasonably-to-be-expected economic benefit of property even if not necessarily to the obvious benefit of the host state." Metalclad, para. 103.

[32] For a review of the relevant case law and Canadian legal principles regarding land use and expropriation see Richard D. Lindgren and Karen Clark, Property Rights vs. Land Use Regulation, Canadian Environmental Law Association, mimeo.

[33] Supreme Court of British Columbia, The United Mexican States and Metalclad Corporation, Reasons for Judgement of the Honourable Mr. Justice Tysoe, May 2, 2001, paragraph 99.

[34] Currently, Alberta is one of only two provinces that charge premiums and premiums account for about 11% of the overall costs of insured services (p. 54).

[35] So while the report expresses "concerns about establishing user fees at the point of service", it encourages regional health authorities to introduce various forms of user fees and co-payments for services on a decentralised basis.

[36] The term "unbundling" is widely used in other service sectors to refer to the splitting apart of vertically-integrated public monopolies into separate functions, which is generally accompanied by re-regulation and privatization. These changes have often been controversial and have sometimes resulted in regulatory chaos. For example, concerns about safety and accountability are prompting the UK government to take steps to re-nationalize the recently "unbundled" and privatized functions of British Rail.

(Barrie Clement, Furious ministers to strip rail chiefs of power, The Independent, 5 January 2004, available at http://news.independent.co.uk/uk/politics/story.jsp?story=478189 , accessed Jan. 5, 2004).

Similarly, "unbundling" and re-regulating the telecommunications industry in the United States is widely seen to have been a public policy failure. A conservative commentator, in an engaging and revealing account of these changes, notes that "implementing the rules has been a logistical nightmare all around." He adds: "Climbing out of this quagmire will be far more difficult than sliding into it." (Peter W. Huber, Telecom Undone—A Cautionary Tale, Manhattan Institute, available free online at http://www.manhattan-institute.org/html/_comm-telecom.htm .

A critical analysis of the plans by Premier Gordon Campbell's Liberal government in British Columbia to "unbundle" and re-regulate the province's electricity industry has recently been released by the Canadian Centre for Policy Alternatives. Marjorie Griffin Cohen, Gutting A Power House: BC Hydro and the new Energy Plan, Canadian Centre for Policy Alternatives, April 2003. (Available at http://www.policyalternatives.ca/bc/gutting-power.pdf , accessed Jan. 5, 2004).

37 U.K. House of Commons Transport Committee, *The Future of the Railway*, Seventh Report of Session 2003-04, Volume I, Report, together with formal minutes, HC 145-1, 1 April 2004. (Available at www.parliament.uk/parliamentary_committees/transport_committee.cfm , accessed April 2, 2004)

For a media assessment of the report, see:

Clement, Barry, "Rail network out of control, say MPs", Independent, April 2, 2004. (Available at http://news.independent.co.uk/uk/transport/story.jsp?story=507513 ; accessed April 2, 2004.)

38 White, Tarina, "CHR ponders rule in U.K. bid," Calgary Herald, September 13, 2003, p. B3.

39 "Setback for flagship government health policy," The Guardian, April 15, 2004.

40 "Calgary may provide health services in the UK," CMAJ, January 20, 2004; 170(2).

41 Carvel, John, "Ministers axe frontrunner in privatised fast-track surgery project," The Guardian, April 16, 2004.

42 Pratt, Sheila, "Private health care not always best value, British experience shows; Klein should take heed before pushing taxpayers down privatization path," *Edmonton Journal*, May 16, 2004.

43 "Setback for flagship government health policy," The Guardian, April 15, 2004, op. cit.

44 Interview with Michael Kirby, Policy Options, December 2002-January 2003, p. 7

45 Ibid., p. 7.

46 Ibid., p. 7.

47 The "meta-analysis" by P.J. Devereaux, et. al. of McMaster University analysed 15 studies to compare mortality rates in investor-owned private for profit hospitals and clinics versus private, not-for-profit institutions. It drew on data covering approximately 38 million patients between 1982 and 1995.

(Devereaux, P.J., et al., "A Systematic Review and Meta-Analysis of Studies Comparing Mortality Rates of Private For-Profit and Private Not-for-Profit Hospitals", in Canadian Medical Association Journal, Vol. 166, No. 11, 28 May 2002, pp.1399-1406.)

48 Their consequent propensity to have reduced highly-skilled staffing levels is, according to the authors, a "likely factor" in their higher death rates. Deveraux, et al. op. cit..

[49] Kirby estimates that "Currently, within Canada's health care system, only 5% of hospital care is delivered by the private for-profit sector."

[50] The Kirby committee appears to base its argument for a reduced role for government on the notion of improved integration of health services through better planning and improved fiscal control.

> "[T]he Committee believes that increased responsibility for decision-making related to the full range of health services, enhanced responsibility for planning and better control over the allocation of resources would lead to greater integration of health services; these are all appropriate roles for R[egional] H[ealth] A[thorities] in the publicly funded health care system today and in the future." (Ch. 3, p. 69)

Curiously, however, the committee does not delve into the issue that such devolution threatens to reduce co-ordination, control and accountability within the overall healthcare system. (See Section 3.1.4)

[51] Laurence, Jeremy, "Private hospitals charging NHS inflated fees for work," The Independent, May 5, 2004.

[52] Note that this proposal, while it seems to be at odds with the Health Care Guarantee proposal, accords with the position of the plaintiffs in the *Chaoulli* Supreme Court case, a position that Senator Kirby has successfully sought intervenor status to support. (See Section 3.2.4)

53 Real or apparent conflicts of interest are likely to arise when senior regional health authority officials have financial interests in private, for-profit clinics and hospitals that contract with the same health authorities. For an analysis of potential conflicts of interest involving private, for-profit surgical facilities and the Calgary Regional Health Authority, see: Gillian Steward, Public Bodies, Private Parts: Surgical contracts and conflicts of interest at the Calgary Regional Health Authority, Parkland Institute, March 2001. (available at http://www.ualberta.ca/PARKLAND/research/studies/ES&PR/ESconflictCRHA.html , accessed Jan. 7, 2004).

54 Stanley H. Hartt, Q.C. and Patrick J. Monahan, *The Charter and Health Care: Guaranteeing Timely Access to Health Care for Canadians*, C.D. Howe Institute, Commentary, No. 164, May 2002. Cited in Kirby, p. 104.

55 The description is from Kirby, p. 107, which cites [2000] J. Q. No. 470 (QL)(C.S.Q. Piche J.), para 243, 261-263.

56 McBane, Michael, "On whose behalf is Senator Kirby speaking?; Senator Kirby and other Senators should withdraw from the case before the Supreme Court," *The Hill Times*, March 22, 2004. (available at http://www.healthcoalition.ca/chaoulli-oped.pdf ; accessed May 14, 2004)

57 Ibid.

58 Response of the Respondent Attorney General of Canada to the Motion for Leave to intervene of Senator Kirby et al. dated December 22, 2003. SCC case 29272. Obtained by fax.

59 Cf. Paul Boothe and Mary Carson, "What Happened to Health Care Reform?", *Commentary*, C.D. Howe Institute, December 2003, p. 5.

[60] While such reforms would find ready support from neo-conservative provincial regimes, presumably they would also be thrust upon even reluctant provincial governments.

[61] Kuttner, Robert, *Everything for Sale: The Virtues and Limits of Markets*, New York: Knopf, 1997, p. 111.

[62] Cf. Section 3.2.4

[63] A recent front page story in the New York Times provides a U.S. example of "gaming" the system. It reports on a new form of back surgery, spinal fusion, which American doctors are administering with increasing frequency. The article points out that there is little evidence that this procedure is better for patients than simpler alternatives, but that the relatively high reimbursement rates from Medicare and Medicaid make it a profitable operation for doctors and hospitals to perform. Reed Abelson and Melody Petersen. "An Operation to Ease Back Pain Bolsters the Bottom Line Too," *New York Times*, December 31, 2003, Page A1, cited in Dean Baker, *Economic Reporting Review*, Janary 5, 2004, available at http://www.cepr.net/pages/Economic_Reporting_Review_Page.htm.

[64] Melody Chen, Outsourcing played role in outbreaks: CDC head, Taipei Times, June 10, 2003, p. 2. (Available at http://www.taipeitimes.com/News/taiwan/archives/2003/06/10/2003054672 , accessed Jan. 6, 2004).

65 See the Canada Health Infoway website at http://www.infoway-inforoute.ca/ , accessed Jan. 6, 2004. It contains specific items on "Alliances with Private Sector" and "Joint Investments". It also contains (at http://www.infoway-inforoute.ca/news-events/index.php?loc=20030331&lang=en , accessed Jan. 6, 2004) a transcript of an interview conducted by David M. Wattling, Managing Partner with Courtyard Group and Founding Chair of CHITTA – Canada's Healthcare Information Technology Trade Association, with Myrna Francis, then Senior Vice-President of Strategic Alliances, Canada Health Infoway. (Francis is currently listed as Interim President and Chief Executive Officer. Prior to joining Infoway, she was General Manager, Health and Life Science Industry at IBM; General Manager of Strategic Business Development in IBM's Healthcare Group; Canadian Managing Partner of CSC Healthcare Group, and held various executive positions in the Ontario government.) As the following excerpts demonstrate, this interview provides Francis' candid perspective on Infoway's partnerships with for-profit companies.

> "Infoway has set an ambitious goal – having the elements of an interoperable HER [Electronic Health Record] across half this country within 7 years. One entity alone cannot accomplish this…."
>
> "We have already met with senior officials from some 30 or 40 companies, comprising IT [information technology] venders and investors. We intend to complement this with an open and ongoing dialog with industry, facilitated by industry groups …"
>
> "To be clear we [Infoway] do not contract directly with the private sector. We do however support projects sponsored by a public sector organization, which may in turn partner with the private sector. The choice of

said partners will be totally up to the public sector sponsor...."

"Infoway will come and it will go. It is here on a very time-limited mission. I am a true believer that things should be left to market forces...."

"I believe healthcare represents the last big vertical market to get into. In fact there is a unique opportunity as the growth in healthcare needs converges with the bust in other sectors. Furthermore Canada represents a great environment in which to build IP and skills, and then sell them into higher priced markets such as the US and Europe."

66 New electronic health record helps keep patients safe, News release and backgrounder, October 21, 2003, Alberta Health and Wellness, Government of Alberta. (available at http://www.gov.ab.ca/acn/200310/15355.html , accessed Jan. 6, 2004)

67 Cited in The Patent Medicines Price Review Board, "Performance Report for the Period Ending March 31, 2002," p. 1. The report is available at http://www.tbs-sct.gc.ca/rma/dpr/01-02/PMPRB/pmprb0102dpr_e.pdf , Cf. Romanow report, Chapter 9, p. 196.

68 Ibid., p. 5.

69 Ibid., p. 5. Data on manufacturers' sales of patented and non-patented drugs is presented, without explanation, in figure 9.4 of the Romanow report (p. 209).

70 Ibid. p. 15.

71 Ouellet, R. 2002. "The Effects of International Trade Agreements on Canadian Health Measures: Options for Canada with a View to the Upcoming Trade Negotiations," Discussion Paper prepared for the Commission on the Future of Health Care in Canada;

Johnson, J.R. 2002. "How Will International Trade Agreements Affect Canadian Health Care?", Discussion Paper prepared for the Commission on the Future of Health Care in Canada.; and

Canadian Centre for Policy Alternatives. 2002. "Globalization and Health: Implications and Options for Health Care Reform." Summary Report by the research consortium from Research Project on Globalization and Health prepared for the Commission on the Future of Health Care in Canada.

72 As indicated in Chapter 4, the extensive and growing involvement of private, for-profit corporations in P3s and in so-called ancillary health care services in Canada raises graver trade treaty risks. However, Romanow's artificial distinction between "direct" and "ancillary" services precludes treatment of this important issue.

73 Strictly speaking, none of these sloppily worded assertions imputed to Romanow are actually expressed as values (i.e. moral standards) such as, "fairness, equity or solidarity" or even as value-statements such as "Canadians consider equal and timely access to medically necessary health care services on the basis of need as a right of citizenship, not a privilege of status or wealth (Romanow, p. xvi)."

74 The website of the Canadian Council for Public-Private Partnerships—an organization of P3 proponents—is found at http://www.pppcouncil.ca , accessed Jan. 7, 2004.

75 Lewis Auerbach, Arthur Donner, Douglas D. Peters, Monica Townson, and Armine Yalnizyan (2003), Funding Hospital Infrastructure: Why P3s Don't Work, and What Will, Canadian Centre for Policy Alternatives, November. (Available at http://www.policyalternatives.ca/publications/p3-hospitals.pdf , accessed Dec. 31, 2003). The quotation is drawn from the authors' open letter to the Ontario Ministers of Health and Long-Term Care, and Public Infrastructure Renewal, which is quoted in a CCPA news release, dated November 6, 2003. (Available at http://www.policyalternatives.ca/whatsnew/p3hospitalspr.html , accessed Dec. 31, 2003).

76 Some of these concerns have been raised by the B.C. Government and Service Employees' Union win connection with the B.C. government's privatization of its Medical Services Plan and Pharmacare systems. (See Section 4.3.3)

Other concerns about the impact of contracting out, or "offshoring", information technology services can be found at:

Addressing the Regulatory Vacuum: Policy Considerations Regarding Public and Private Sector Service Job Offshoring, Public Citizen, available at http://www.citizen.org/documents/OffshoringReport.pdf .

77 Clark, Thomas, "Hospitals offer a prescription for profit," *Financial Times of London*, February 10, 2004.

78 In accordance with this recommendation of the Mazankowski Report, the Alberta government established an Expert Advisory Panel to Review Publicly Funded Health Services in May 2002. Its stated purpose was "to review the current basket of publicly funded health services and, on an ongoing basis, to review new health services to ensure that Alberta's publicly funded health services remain comprehensive and sustainable for the future, and provide the best value." (Panel's Progress Report to December 2002, p. 1).

The panel's initial Progress Report, issued in December 2002, recommended the Alberta government reduce, review or restrict funding for four services: optometry services, podiatry services, chiropractic services, and community physical therapy provided outside of hospitals. These services are not now covered by the *Canada Health Act* but are covered by Alberta's public insurance plan.

More generally, the panel concluded that "the categories of services [it was provided] are too broad to allow a useful analysis of whether or not funding should be continued for each category of services." (p. 29) It recommended that "funding should be continued for the broad categories currently in place" but that this does not mean "that all services within those broad categories should continue to be funded." (p. 29). The panel asserted that "a complete review ... is critical" – a task the panel stated it was unable to accomplish "[g]iven the timeframes involved." (p. 29)

The panel also concluded that

> "the only way to make decisions about continued funding for currently-funded services is to set criteria for deciding which of these services warrant review, to establish priorities, then review specific services that match the criteria. This process would allow the Panel to determine whether or not funding should be continued and, perhaps more importantly, under what conditions funding should be provided. As a result, the Panel will proceed to develop criteria to identify high priority, currently funded health services that would be reviewed on an ongoing basis, using the process and structure developed [by the Panel] ...." (pp. 29-30)

The panel's final report, issued in March 2003, provides a model for assessing publicly funded health services and technologies. It recommends review process consisting of a technical screen, a social and economic screen, and a fiscal screen.

On July 18, 2003, Alberta Minister of Health and Wellness Gary Mar outlined the provincial government's response to the two panel reports in a news release. According to the Hon. Mar, the reports "recommended maintaining the currently funded categories of health services" – a finding the government accepted. (para. 2) However, the government rejected the panel's recommended funding reductions and other changes to optometry, podiatry, chiropractic services and community physical therapy services. The Minister also indicated that the government accepted "in principle" the panel's recommended "process to assess which new and emerging health services should be covered publicly," though it would "work with existing resources" rather than "create another advisory board, as proposed." (para. 4).

Expert Advisory Panel to Review Publicly Funded Health Services, Progress Report to December 2002, Alberta Health and Wellness, 40 pp. (Available at http://www.health.gov.ab.ca/reform/EAPprogress.pdf , accessed Dec. 29, 2003).

The Burden of Proof: An Alberta Model for Assessing Publicly Funded Health Services, Final Report of the Expert Panel to Review Publicly Funded Health Services, March, 2003, 28 pp. (Available at http://www.health.gov.ab.ca/reform/EAPprocess.pdf , accessed Dec. 29, 2003).

"Government funding right health services now, focus on new process for funding future services," News Release, Alberta Health and Wellness, Government of Alberta, July 18, 2003. Available at http://www.gov.ab.ca/acn/200307/14802.html , accessed Dec. 29, 2003).

[79] The GATS national treatment and market access provisions apply only to those sectors that each government has listed in its country schedule. As noted in Chapter 2, these listed commitments are referred to as specific commitments.

[80] Canadian Centre for Policy Alternatives, *Putting Health First, supra,* Chapter 2, endnote 1.

[81] Canada, Schedule of Specific Commitments, supplement 4, 26 February 1998.

82 In Q&As on its public web site the federal Department of International Trade (formerly DFAIT) admits this issue, stating: "Question: 'What about private health insurance in the GATS?' Answer: 'In 1997, Canada made market access and national treatment commitments with respect to private health insurance such as that provided by Blue Cross. Commitments made on private health insurance do not undermine or require us to change our public health insurance system.' Question: 'What if the Government decides to expand public health insurance?' Answer: 'Should Canadian governments decide to expand public health insurance to areas previously covered by private health insurance, *the GATS has procedures to modify our commitments as necessary.'* (emphasis added)," (http://strategis.ic.gc.ca/epic/internet/instp-pcs.nsf/en/h_sk00152e.html ; accessed May 1, 2004)

83 See: Mathew Sanger, *Reckless Abandon: Canada the GATS and the Future of Health Care*, Canadian Centre for Policy Alternatives, 2001, esp. pp. 77-89;

Putting Health First, op. cit, p. 25, and

Johnson, J.R. 2002. 'How will international trade agreements affect Canadian healthcare,' Draft discussion paper prepared for the Commission for the Future of Health Care in Canada. , pp. 18-19.

84 These assertions are considered in greater detail in *Putting Health First*, Canadian Centre for Policy Alternatives, 2002, op. cit., pp. 12-14.

85 GATS Article I:3.c.

86 For a critical examination of the GATS "governmental authority" exclusion, see Perilous Lessons, op. cit., pp. 24-29 and 85, where this indirect effect is considered.

[87] As noted in Perilous Lessons, this analysis is based on the generous assumption, perhaps unwarranted, that the GATS "governmental authority" exclusion provides some degree of meaningful protection. (Ibid., Chapter 3, endnote 48).

[88] It should be noted, however, that the NAFTA national treatment obligations does not apply to subsidies (NAFTA Art. 1108.7).

[89] A vital legal case on public health care has now gone to the Supreme Court of Canada. In Jacques Chaoulli et al. v. Attorney General of Quebec, Dr. Chaoulli and George Zeliotis are seeking to overturn a Quebec court decision that prohibited the latter from paying privately for a hip replacement. The two argue that the decision violates the right to life, liberty and security under the Charter of Rights and Freedoms.

As noted in Section 3.2.4, Senator Kirby and other members of the Kirby committee filed a motion for leave to intervene on December 10, 2003, and on May 4, 2004 were granted leave to present oral argument in their individual capacity. Other notable organizations have filed responses, notices of intervention, or motions for leave to intervene in this important case. These include the federal and a number of provincial attorneys general, the Canadian Medical Association, the Canadian Labour Congress, the Canadian Health Coalition, and a number of private, for-profit surgery and health services corporations.

The Supreme Court docket and related information for this case is available on the Supreme Court web site at http://www.scc-csc.gc.ca/Welcome/index_e.asp . Select "cases", then "SCC Case Information" and search for "29272". (Accessed Jan. 6, 2004 and May 18, 2004).

90 For example, government action to reduce tobacco use is but one of a range of measures that would likely be far more significant in improving health outcomes among Canadians.

Recent research in the U.K. found that many computer systems used by general practitioners failed to detect dangerous prescribing errors.

Moss, Lyndsay, "GPs' computers 'risking lives,'" *The Independent*, May 14, 2004. (available at http://news.independent.co.uk/uk/health_medical/story.jsp?story=521087 ; accessed May 14, 2004)

91 Mahoney, Jill, "Klein issues medicare threat," *Globe and Mail*, February 20, 2004.

Premier Klein was also quoted as stating:

"Maybe now, we've got to do the un-Canadian thing and take on the *Canada Health Act* in order to achieve sustainability in the health-care system."

Baxter, James, "Time to be 'un-Canadian'; Klein to fight election over challenge to *Canada Health Act*," *The Edmonton Journal*, March 19, 2004.

92 Dix, Adrian, "Let's spend on health care, not on ads," Victoria *Times Colonist*, January 18, 2004.

93 Premier Campbell was quoted as saying that since Martin was in power, "it may well turn out that we don't need it [passage of the bill] at all."

Kennedy, Mark, "Liberals softening stance on Medicare rules: critics," *Ottawa Citizen* and *Vancouver Sun*, April 27, 2004. (available at http://www.healthcoalition.ca/kennedy-pettigrew.html ; accessed May 14, 2004)

[94] Griffin Cohen, Marjorie and Cohen, Marcy, A Return to Wage Discrimination: Pay Equity Losses Through the Privatization of Health Care, Canadian Centre for Policy Alternatives, April 2004 (available at http://www.policyalternatives.ca ; accessed May 12, 2004)

[95] Gordon, Mary, "Health Minister open to 'options'; Wants for-profit services explored; Remarks draw fire from critics," *Toronto Star*, April 28, 2004.

[96] Ibid.

[97] Kennedy, Mark, "Liberals softening stance on Medicare rules: critics," *Ottawa Citizen* and *Vancouver Sun*, April 27, 2004, op. cit. (available at http://www.healthcoalition.ca/kennedy-pettigrew.html ; accessed May 14, 2004)

[98] Ibid.

[99] Ibid.

[100] Bueckert, Dennis, "Federal government fights judicial review of its record defending medicare," Canadian Press, May 10, 2004. (available at http://www.healthcoalition.ca/cha_suit_may10.pdf ; accessed May 14, 2004)

[101] Gordon, Mary, "Health Minister open to 'options'; Wants for-profit services explored; Remarks draw fire from critics," *Toronto Star*, April 28, 2004, op. cit..

[102] Kennedy, Mark, "Pettigrew flip-flops to election tune," *Ottawa Citizen*, April 29, 2004. (available at http://www.healthcoalition.ca/retraction.pdf ; accessed May 14, 2004)

[103] "No private delivery of health care: Pettigrew," CBC Website, April 28, 2004.

[104] Smith, Graeme, "PM urges lasting health-care change; Martin, Goodale deflect flak on funding, demand co-operation from provinces," *Globe and Mail*, March 27, 2004.

See also:

Laghi, Brian, "Martin to offer provinces new deal on health," *Globe and Mail*, April 16, 2004.

[105] Website, Public-Private Partnership (P3) Office, Industry Canada. (http://strategis.ic.gc.ca/epic/internet/inpupr-bdpr.nsf/en/Home ; accessed May 14, 2004)

[106] Curry, Bill, "Privatization deals 'the way government is going to be done'; Federal projects, services, PS jobs, to be handed over to private sector," *Ottawa Citizen*, February 9, 2004.

[107] Ibid.

[108] Ibid.

[109] Ibid.

[110] In a disconcerting refrain of the Mazankowski report's reference to "the old 'command and control' central planning approach" (see Section 3.1.3), McKay is quoted as using even more extreme language in expounding a similar perspective:

"'I anticipate that (reaction) [by opponents against privatizing health care services],' said McKay. 'But they're locked in the Marxist-Leninist dialogue of the 1960s and 70s and I feel sorry for them. Because the choice is not between same old, same old government doing things the way they've been doing it and P3s. The choice is P3 or nothing and Canadians are going to have to face the issue: Why does a public entity have to own the hospital? Why does a public entity have to finance a hospital?'"

Curry, Bill, "Liberals building a case for privatizing: PM's point man says, 'This is the way government is going to be done,'" *National Post*, February 9, 2004, p. A1.

111 Ibid.

112 Naumetz, Tim, "Private health advocate joints Martin team: Critics fear major shift in policy as PM shuffles senior ranks," *Ottawa Citizen*, April 9, 2004. (Available at http://www.healthcarecoalition.ca/boothe.pdf ; access May 14, 2004)

113 Boothe, Paul, and Carson, Mary, "What Happened to Health-Care Reform," *Commentary*, C.D. Howe Institute, No. 193, December 2003. (Available at http://www.cdhow.org/pdf/commentary_193.pdf ; accessed May 17, 2004)

114 Ibid., p. 16.

115 Tieleman, Bill, "Political Connections; Liberal Lobbyist Lands in the PM's Office," *Georgia Straight*, February 12, 2004. (Available at http://www.straight.com/content.cfm?id=794 ; accessed May 17, 2004)

116 Inventory of Major Privatization Initiatives in the Canadian Health Care System 2003-2004 (updated April 2004), compiled by Corina Crawley, Canadian Union of Public Employees (available at http://www.cupe.ca/updir/HCInventory-Revised-APRIL_Version2004.pdf; accessed May 26, 2004).

117 The new federal administration, headed by Liberal Prime Minister Paul Martin, has mounted no new initiatives to curb health care commercialization in Canada. Instead, the Prime Minister signalled a disturbing predilection P3s with the announcement that Scarborough East M.P. John McKay's new job as Parliamentary Secretary to the Minister of Finance included a "special emphasis on Public Private Partnerships." (http://www1.pm.gc.ca/eng/new_team_1.asp , accessed Jan. 17, 2004).

118 This consortium consists of Brookfield Lepage Johnson Controls (BLJC), the Canadian branch of Amsterdam-based ABN Ambro Bank N.V., and Edmonton-based PCL Construction Group. (Cf. Privatization Poachers: The Four Consortia, *Guardian*, Hospital Employees' Union, Volume 21, Issue 3, October 2003. (available on www.heu.org; accessed March 4, 2004)

119 Leslie, Tricia, "Only one bidder left to build new hospital," *Abbotsford Times*, February 10, 2004, p. 7.

120 "New 'value for money' assessment warranted as costs climb, significant changes made to Abbotsford P3 hospital project—Parks' RFP review," Hospital Employees' Union news release, February 25, 2004. (available on http://www.heu.org ; accessed March 4, 2004)

121 Cf Derfel, Kevin, "Keep private sector out of superhospitals: MDs; Lobby group foresees higher costs. Physicians for Social Justice criticizes report by Mulroney-Johnson commission," *The Gazette* (Montreal), April 20, 2004, p. A7.

122 Government of Ontario, McGuinty Brings New Ottawa and Brampton Hospitals Into Public Hands; Affirms commitment to publicly owned, controlled and accountable hospitals, News Release, November 21, 2003.

Thomas Walkom, McGuinty's credibility at stake; Voters tolerant at first but not forever, *Toronto Star*, November 25, 2003.

P3 by any other name, Editorial, *Toronto Star*, November 26, 2003.

123 "Newly Released Documents Confirm Massive Hospital Privatization—All Financial Information Withheld By Government," News release, Ontario Health Coalition, March 15, 2004. (available at http://www.web.net/~ohc/040315.htm ; accessed May 12, 2004)

124 Keith Leslie, Unions warn more privately funded hospitals will hurt universal medicare, Canadian Press, January 12, 2004. (available at http://www.canada.com/vancouver/story.asp?id=94DAEBF5-858E-4C21-8370-5C0D4A6541C5) See also: Liberal accused of secret P3 planning; Six more private hospitals planned for Ontario, unions charge, Toronto Star, January 12, 2004, (available at http://www.torontostar.com/NASApp/cs/ContentServer?pagename=thestar/Layout/Article_Type1&c=Article&cid=1073905596555&call_pageid=968332188492&col=968705899037 ; both accessed Jan. 12, 2004).

125 Boyle, Theresa, "Activists fear P3 hospital program; 'May be brought in the back door' Six hospitals eye private financing," *Toronto Star*, January 13, 2004, p. A6.

126 Brennan, Richard and Benzie, Robert, "More P3 schemes possible: Liberals; There could be room for private sector, But no more hospitals planned, Smitherman says," *Toronto Star*, April 12, 2004. (available at http://www.thestar.com/NASApp/cs/ContentServer?pagename=thestar/Layout/Article_Type1&call_pageid=971358637177&c=Article&cid=1081462213364 ; accessed April 12, 2004)

127 Partnerships British Columbia, Academic Ambulatory Care Centre, Fact Sheet, December 2003. (http://www.partnershipsbc.com/pdf/aac_fact_sheet.pdf ; accessed Jan. 17, 2004).

128 Don Harrison, Suits plague firm tipped to run kidney care, The Province, March 27, 2003, p. A34.

> The company has also acknowledged to the U.S. Securities and Exchange Commission that it has been named in nine lawsuits alleging the company artificially inflated the price of drugs bought under the U.S. government's subsidized health care system for the poor. (Ibid.)

129 Joanne Laucius, Footing the bill for health care: People are becoming medical consumers, paying for everything from PSA scans to acupuncture, March 22, 2003, Vancouver Sun, p. B6.

130 Paula Simons, Private Hospital won't provide cure for waiting lists elsewhere: Health authorities could lose dollars to new facility, September 24, 2002, Edmonton Journal, p. B1;

> Private surgical facility approved for uninsured overnight stays, Carstairs Courier, September 24, 2002, p. 4.

131 Chapman, Sarah, "Health centre expected to cut ER wait times," *Calgary Herald*, January 19, 2004, p. B3.

132 Barbara Kermode-Scott, "Alberta region pushes privatization," *Medical Post*, Vol. 39, No. 32, September 9, 2003, p.61.

David Heynan, "CHR expands private clinic strategy: Diagnostic waits targeted," Calgary Herald, July 13, 2003, p. A1.

133 Theresa Boyle, "Addiction, mental health sites may be merged; Private sector key part of $382M plan Queen St. facility would be central site," *Toronto Star*, July 10, 2003, p. A1.

The report states:

"The Centre for Addiction and Mental Health (CAMH) is pursuing a plan to allow the private sector to rebuild, equip and lease back to the Ontario government a central site at its existing Queen Street facility.

"A copy of a confidential communications memo, obtained by the Star, acknowledges 'much criticism' over public-private partnerships—or P3s as they are known—and advises hospital brass shift attention away from the thorny issue."

134 For the government's description of the arrangement and events, see:

"MSP Service Delivery Model to Improve Client Service," News Release, Ministry of Health Services, March 31, 2004. (Available at http://www2.news.gov.bc.ca/nrm_news_releases/2004HSER0016-000224.htm# ; accessed May 17, 2004)

and

British Columbia Medical Services Plan website, http://www.healthservices.gov.bc.ca/msp/ ; accessed May 17, 2004.

135 See "BCGEU asks court to review legality of privatizing MSP", News Release, B.C. Government and Service Employees' Union, February 24, 2004. (Available at http://www.bcgeu.ca/2076 ; accessed May 17, 2004)

and

"Stop privatization of MSP and Pharmacare until privacy concerns answered, union urges government," News Release, B.C. Government and Service Employees' Union, March 31, 2004. (Available at http://www.bcgeu.ca/2088 ; accessed May 17, 2004)

For the BCGEU legal documents concerning the MSP privatization, go to http://www.bcgeu.ca/2093 ; accessed May 17, 2004)

136 The text of the bill is available, in English, at http://www.publicationsduquebec.gouv.qc.ca/dynamicSearch/telecharge.php?type=5&file=2003C26A.PDF , accessed Jan. 2, 2004.

137 The following media reports provide additional information about the controversial bill passed by Premier Jean Charest's Liberal government in December:

Allison Hanes, "Charest vows no retreat, Blasts tactics. Labour leaders warn of more disruptions", The Gazette, December 3, 2003.

"Quebec legislature sits all night as government forces through series of laws", Canadian Press, December 17, 2003.

Les Perreaux, "Quebec's stormy labour scene will heat up even more in spring 2004", Canadian Press, December 27, 2003.

138 Brennan, Richard and Benzie, Robert, "More P3 schemes possible: Liberals; There could be room for private sector, But no more hospitals planned, Smitherman says," *Toronto Star*, April 12, 2004, op. cit.. (available at http://www.thestar.com/NASApp/cs/ContentServer?pagename=thestar/Layout/Article_Type1&call_pageid=971358637177&c=Article&cid=1081462213364 ; accessed April 12, 2004)

139 The text of the amended bill is available at http://www.ontla.on.ca/documents/Bills/38_Parliament/Session1/b008rep_e.pdf , accessed May 17, 2004.

140 The bill was considered by the Standing Committee on Justice and Social Policy on May 3, 4, 10, and 11, where it was amended.

141 Provisions that would also have given the Minister the authority to make unilateral changes to existing health care contracts and agreements were removed by amendments. (cf. Sack Goldblatt Mitchell, Analysis of the Effect of Bill 8 Amendments on the Validity and Enforceability of Collective Agreements, March 12, 2004. (Available at http://www.cupe.ca/www/bill8campaign/9319 ; accessed May 17, 2004))

142 Note, however, that this would not preclude U.S. (or Mexican) corporations or affiliates from seeking compensation for cancelled P3s under NAFTA's investment provisions.

143 Broadcast News, Yorkton, Saskatchewan – A private personal care home's move to Yorkton, Saskatchewan is raising questions at a public sector union, December 5, 2002.

Sheri Trapp, Region clarifies position on care homes, Yorkton This Week and Enterprise, December 18, 2002, p. A1.

144 Paul McKay, "Taxpayers finance construction boom: Over the next 20 years, Ontario will heavily subsidize the construction and renovation of thousands of nursing home beds in the province. As Paul McKay reports, a company controlled by the Reichmann family is the single biggest beneficiary, April 29, 2003, The Ottawa Citizen, p. A11.

145 According to Georgia Straight reporter Charlie Smith, Compas, Sodexho and Aramark are members of the Canadian Council for Public-Private Partnerships.

Smith, Charlie, "Union leaders' firm backed B.C. Liberals," *Georgia Straight*, May 13, 2004. (available at http://www.straight.com/content.cfm?id=2644 ; accessed May 13, 2004)

146 Ontario Health Coalition, Briefing Note on Carrillion and P3 Controversies, February 24, 2004. (available at http://www.web.net/~ohc/carillion.htm ; accessed May 12, 2004)

Se also, "Carillion: Profile of a Privateer", Canadian Union of Public Employees, undated. (available on http://www.cupe.ca ; accessed March 4, 2004.)

147 "The Facts: on The Compass Group—a New Player in Privatized Food Services," Canadian Union of Public Employees, June 10, 2001. (available at http://www.cupe.ca/www/corporateprofiles/4328 ; accessed May 12, 2004)

148 Walker, Tom, "Privateer Watch: Who is Sodexho?," Research report prepared for the Hospital Employees' Union, The B.C. Health Services Division of the Canadian Union of Public Employees, May 1, 2002. (available at http://www.cupe.ca/updir/sodexho_profile.pdf ; accessed May 12, 2004)

149 Cf. "BC housekeeping privatization bad news for workers, patients," Canadian Union of Public Employees, July 30, 2003. (available at http://www.cupe.ca/www/57/ART3f2825fbb069f ; accessed May 12, 2004)

See also: http://www.aramark.ca .

For information on Aramark's involvement in cost overruns in food service centralization (P3) projects in Winnipeg-area hospitals, see the reports prepared by the Manitoba Auditor General (2000-1) and the Canadian Centre for Policy Alternatives at http://www.oag.mb.ca/reports/reports_fr.htm and http://www.policyalternatives.ca/manitoba/foodpr.html respectively.

150 Some of these points are drawn from *Perilous Lessons*, op. cit., p. 106-120.

151 Troublingly, some influential observers have celebrated the role that international treaty negotiations can play in permitting governments to make changes that otherwise would prove politically untenable—in other words, in enabling governments to make politically unpopular decisions by stealth. In the context of international negotiations on services, the WTO Secretariat has stated:

"[T]here are various economic and political advantages associated with liberalization commitments under the GATS ... [including] ... *[o]vercoming domestic resistance to change...*"

One prominent WTO official went so far as to imply that GATS commitments provided governments a valuable means to evade the democratic will of its citizens. He likened governments' GATS commitments "to Ulysses' decision to have himself tied to the mast in order to resist the sirens." This disturbing view was also espoused by the then-director of the WTO services division, David Hartridge, with respect to telecommunications:

"[c]ountries which want and badly need investment ... can use the negotiations as a way of circumventing vested interests which may not favour liberalization."

Sources:

World Trade Organization, *Services: GATS*, Training Package, December 1998, p. 57.

Rolf Adlung, WTO Secretariat, Trade in Services Division, The Political Economy of Adjusting to Services Trade Liberalization: Developed and Developing Country Perspectives. Adlung cites Frieder Roessler as first using the metaphor, in: The Scope, Limits and Function of the GATT Legal System, World Economy, Vol. 8, no. 3, 1985, p. 287. Sinclair, 2000 (op. cit., p. 65, endnote 87) notes that "Mr. Adlung invokes this metaphor as capturing "the *domestic* policy rationale" for arguing in favour of multilateral liberalization (emphasis in original).

Hartridge, David, What the General Agreement on Trade in Services (GATS) Can Do, in *Opening markets for Banking Worldwide: The WTO General Agreement on Trade in Services,* Proceedings of a conference organized by British Invisibles and Clifford Chance that was held in London, U.K, on 8 January 1997. The proceedings were originally available at http://www.1999.cliffordchance.com/library/publications/wto/section3.html

but no longer appear on that site.

152 Sinclair and Grieshaber-Otto (2002), op. cit..

153 This section draws heavily upon Sinclair (2000), Sinclair and Grieshaber-Otto (2002), and Grieshaber-Otto and Sanger (2002).

154 Article VI:4, emphasis added.

155 World Trade Organization, Working Party on Professional Services, "The Relevance of the Disciplines of the Agreements on Technical Barriers to Trade and on Import Licensing to Article VI.4 of the GATS," Note by the Secretariat, 11 September 1996 (S/WPPS/W/9). Cited in Sinclair and Grieshaber-Otto, 2002, op. cit..

156 In a paper prepared for a recent OECD/US forum on trade in educational services, GATS proponent Pierre Sauvé emphasizes the importance of the GATS domestic regulation provisions:

> "[T]he GATS could play a useful role … in ensuring that regulatory measures in this area … even while non-discriminatory in character, are not unduly burdensome or indeed disguised restrictions to trade and investment in the sector. The adoption of possible disciplines on domestic regulation … and in particular the adoption of a necessity test … could be important in this regard, though one cannot underestimate the political sensitivities that lie ahead in this area."
>
> (Pierre Sauvé, *Trade, Education and the GATS*, op. cit., p. 28.)

157 In sharp contrast to other clauses in Article VI, subsection 4 does not contain language that would limit its application to "sectors in which a Member has undertaken specific commitments".

158 Sinclair and Grieshaber-Otto, 2002, op. cit..

159 Ministerial Declaration, Free Trade Area of the Americas Eighth Ministerial Meeting, Miami, U.S.A., November 20, 2003, para. 10.

160 "Free Trade in the Americas," SELA Antenna in the United States, No. 68, 3rd quarter 2003.

161 The November 1, 2002 drafts of the FTAAA services and investment chapters are available at http://www.dfait-maeci.gc.ca/tna-nac/ftaa_neg-en.asp .

162 For a helpful discussion which clearly distinguishes between the role of the private sector in financing and delivery, see the note by Steve Morgan: What role should the private sector play in health care?, Centre for Health Services and Policy Research, University of British Columbia, Nov. 13, 2000.

163 Robert G. Evans, Morris L. Barer, Steven Lewis, Michael Rachlis, and Greg L. Stoddart, Private Highway, One-way Street: The De-Klein and Fall of Canadian Medicare?, Centre for Health Services and Policy Research, University of British Columbia, March 2000.

164 As previously noted, so-called ancillary services range from food services, cleaning services, laundry services, maintenance services, accounting services, computer and data management services, security services, accounting services, management services and many other crucial components of the health care delivery system.

165 The Alberta government even commissioned a legal opinion on the matter, which it publicly released.

166 Romanow report, Ch. 11, p. 255.

167 Romanow report, Ch. 1, p. 9.

168 For example, only two major US health insurers are currently active in the Canadian private health insurance market: Liberty Health, a Canadian unit of Liberty Mutual Insurance Co. of Boston and Maritime Life Assurance Co, a subsidiary of John Hancock Financial Services, also of Boston. US insurers estimate their share of the Canadian private insurance market at less than 10 per cent. This market share, however, could increase rapidly through competition or a possible takeover of a Canadian insurer. See Paul Knox, "Do International Trade Agreements Threaten Medicare?" *Globe and Mail*, December 6, 2002.

169 Romanow report, Ch. 11, p. 238.

170 Canadian Centre for Policy Alternatives, 2002, *Putting Health First*, op. cit., p. ix.

171 Canadian Centre for Policy Alternatives, 2002, *Putting Health First*, op. cit. p. v.

172 Ibid.

173 In May 2003 the Canadian Union of Public Employees; the Communications Energy and Paperworkers Union of Canada; the Canadian Health Coalition; the Canadian Federation of Nurses Unions; and the Council of Canadians filed an application in the Federal Court of Canada seeking declarations that the Minister of Health is failing to monitor and enforce the *Canada Health Act* and seeking an order from the Court requiring the Minister to do so. The organizations' witnesses have sworn affidavits detailing the ways that the federal government has been negligent in enforcing the *Canada Health Act*. Information on the case is available on the Canada Health Coalition website; a two page explanatory summary of the case is at http://www.healthcoalition.ca/case.pdf (accessed Jan. 8, 2004).

174 One prominent Canadian trade lawyer has argued that, "If this provision [NAFTA Article 1110, Expropriation and Compensation] and the accompanying investor/state dispute settlement procedures had existed in the 1960s, the public health care system in its present form would never have come into existence."

(Jon Johnson, How will international trade agreements affect Canadian health care?, Commission on the Future of Health Care in Canada, Discussion paper 22, September 2002.)

175 For example, a prohibition of monopolies and the application of national treatment to subsidies, neither of which is a NAFTA feature.

176 Canada's current position is that it will make no GATS requests of others to cover direct health services, but Canada continues to press other countries to cover health insurance and other health-related services where Canada has already made GATS commitments.

177 The human right to health is embodied in customary and conventional (treaty) law, as well as in a variety of international agreements, declarations and plans of action. ... notably the right to health as treated in the International Covenant on Economic, Social and Cultural Rights to which Canada is a state party. See: Chantal Blouin, John Foster, and Ronald Labonte, Canada's Foreign Policy and Health: Toward Policy Coherence, Commission on the Future of Health Care in Canada, 2002.